BORN TOO SOON

A Guide To Coping With Preterm Birth in Africa

ALEX AND STELLA MOKORI

Kemp House
152-160 City Road
London, EC1V 2NX
United Kingdom

ISBN: 978-1-917003-69-8

Published by Alex Mokori, Stella Mokori and Action Wealth
    Publishing
Printed and bound in the United Kingdom

To God Almighty, for the gift of salvation and eternal life, and above all, for making us co-creators with Him in receiving the precious gift of our special baby, Jair.

We dedicate this book to Jair and the many other preemies who have overcome the odds to share their stories.

We also honor the dedicated healthcare professionals, parents, caregivers and the entire social support machinery who tirelessly work to save the lives of preterm infants every day.

৯৶৯৶৯৶৯৶৯৶

CONTENTS

∽∽∽∽∽

ACKNOWLEDGMENTS

We acknowledge our parents, relatives, friends, and colleagues who never gave up on us during trying situations. Your unwavering support and encouragement have been invaluable, and your place in our lives will forever remain cherished. You are truly a blessing.

To all the medical and healthcare workers in International Hospital Kampala (IHK) and Lynwood Medical Center, Nsasa in Kira who have walked this journey with us from prenatal care through the challenges of maternity and into postnatal care and beyond we extend our deepest gratitude. Each of you has played a crucial role in our lives and in caring for our precious baby. Your dedication, compassion, and expertise have been a beacon of hope and strength during our most challenging times.

Special thanks to the doctors, nurses, midwives, nutritionists, lactation consultants, and support staff who provided exceptional care and support. Your tireless efforts, seen and unseen, have made a profound difference in our journey. May the good Lord richly bless you all for your kindness, commitment, and the lifesaving work you do every day.

Many thanks to the subject matter experts, especially Dr. Elizabeth Kiboneka, a retired Ugandan

Consultant Paediatrician, for her review of this book and guidance. Also, to all professional colleagues in the Ministry of Health, UNICEF, and professional networks whose input made this work possible.

We also extend our heartfelt thanks to the Ministries of Health, healthcare institutions,, and training centers that strive to build the competencies of healthcare professionals and ensure that every mother and preterm baby receives the best possible care.

This book is a testament to the power of community, faith, and the indomitable human spirit. Thank you all for being a part of our story and helping us navigate this extraordinary journey.

⤜⤜⤜⤜⤜⤜

PREFACE

Preterm birth presents a unique set of challenges, not only for the newborns fighting to survive and thrive but also for their families, healthcare professionals, governments, implementing partners, and the private sector who must contend with its enormous costs. It is, indeed, a full societal issue. The journey through preterm birth is often fraught with uncertainty, fear, and emotional turbulence, yet it is also a journey marked by resilience, hope, and the unwavering strength of the human spirit.

This book is born out of our personal experience with preterm birth and our desire to shed light on the complexities and triumphs associated with it. It stands as a testament to the incredible resilience of preterm babies, the unwavering dedication of healthcare professionals, and the profound support from family, friends, and colleagues.

We wrote this book to provide a comprehensive guide for parents, caregivers, and healthcare professionals navigating the often-overwhelming world of preterm care. Our goal is to share insights, provide practical advice, and offer encouragement to those facing similar journeys. Additionally, it serves as a call to action for governments, development partners, civil society organizations, professional associations, and the private sector to create a conducive environment and provide support to prevent and care for preterm babies and their families. The statistics are grim, and the impact on the economy, community, and family is immense.

In developing countries, particularly in sub-Saharan Africa, the role of registered nutritionists and dietitians in maternal and newborn care is not well recognized, both in the private sector and government facilities where most preterm deliveries occur. Specialty training in lactation counseling and support in neonatal intensive care units (NICUs) and post-discharge is almost non-existent. It is crucial for both government and private sectors to incorporate registered nutritionists and dietitians as part of the core care team, enhancing the quality of care for preterm infants. It's also important to have these cadres empowered to provide nutrition and dietary support to mothers to reduce the incidence of preterm and low birth weight births in Africa.

Healthcare training institutes play a pivotal role in building the competencies of nutritionists, dietitians, and other healthcare professionals, equipping them with the skills needed to support preterm babies and their families. We advocate for an increased focus on specialized training to ensure that every preterm baby receives the best possible nutritional support. This need extends to doctors, nurses, and midwives in both rural and urban areas. We require a dedicated mass of professionals to support preterm care and prevent unnecessary deaths, especially in resource-constrained settings.

There is also a need to address the critical role of human breast milk banks, which are essential for the nourishment of preterm infants. Unfortunately, these facilities are lacking in many African countries, and there is no policy guidance to support them. This is, therefore, a call on governments, development partners, the private sector, and the general public to recognize the importance of breast milk banks and take action to establish and support these vital facilities. We also urge mothers to donate safe breast milk to help save the lives of preterm babies. In Uganda, for instance, St. Francis Hospital Nsambya, Nakasero Hospital, and Mbale Regional Referral Hospital have taken commendable steps in establishing breast milk banks among others, but the journey is only beginning for Uganda.

This book brings out a blend of scientific information, personal anecdotes, and practical tips designed to inform and support you. Whether you are a parent of a preterm baby, a healthcare professional, a government official, a development partner representative, or someone interested in understanding preterm care, we hope this book provides valuable insights and encouragement.

We dedicate this book to all the preterm babies who have fought and continue to fight for their lives to thrive, the healthcare professionals who dedicate their lives to saving these precious souls, and the families who show immense courage and love in the face of adversity. Together, we can make a difference and ensure that every preterm baby has the best possible start in life.

✦✦✦✦✦

INTRODUCTION

As first-timers, the news of our pregnancy brought us the greatest joy and a boundless blessing. We were young, able, and excelling in our personal and professional pursuits.

But somewhere around 33 weeks into the pregnancy, something went wrong, and Stella was given shocking news and pressured choices after a call from her gynecologist. She was told that the baby had stopped growing inside her womb (a medical condition known as intrauterine growth retardation IUGR)[1] and that the only option was an emergency operation to deliver our baby. This was a life-changing event for our baby and ourselves and was the start of several challenging months where we learned, loved, hoped, prayed, and followed medical advice and instructions

---

[1] Throughout this book, we will use the term preterm to refer collectively to the three key conditions of small vulnerable newborns (SVNs): being born too soon (preterm), being born too small due to fetal growth restriction (small for gestational age, or SGA), and being born with low birthweight. All three conditions were present in our son.

so that our baby could survive and grow well without any long-term physical, mental, or psycho-social complications. This book accounts for one of the most trying periods for a mother (often single and alone) and a father. But it is also for anyone else who has faced, is, or will face a similar situation.

We realized the impact preterm birth and delivery had on the rest of the family and support system, given that the birth of a baby is of great significance in some cultures and traditions, with specific rituals and customs being performed. When the baby is born preterm, this changes much of that and must be addressed. Even the fact that the baby is born small is more fragile, and it often battles compromised immunity; thus, being unable to have visitors for months can become an issue for the family and loved ones. As new parents, this was unforeseen, and we had to navigate these challenges while prioritizing the well-being of our baby, which was at the center of everything else.

We were not prepared for the emotional rollercoaster ride that we were taken on without warning. From highs of pride, relief, and joy, we would meet despondency and fear on the way down some days. We learned to start each day with renewed faith and a willingness to do whatever it would take to have our baby grow well. We were even less ready for the many preconceived ideas and intergenerational challenges relating to preterm births, which we hope will be addressed through our sharing our story in as much detail as we can. We desire to help other parents, grandparents, caregivers, and custodians to get to the other side of a preterm pregnancy and onward to sustained care and well-being. Sadly, there is still a fair amount of blame, guilt, and shame associated with an early-born baby or preemie as they are fondly known. Mothers are also anxiously replying about what they could have done better, and parents, in-laws, friends, workmates, and neighbors are adding their two cents about what should have been done. The mother is too short or doesn't eat, rest, or take sufficient supplements. They are not fit enough because they have difficulty not doing enough manual labor as women do in rural areas. Similarly, fathers have their share of the blame, such as neglect of the wife, the source of the wife's stress, or sheer being married to work. On and off goes the list of "If Onlys" and "They should've known betters." We believe more information could be helpful to strengthen the support networks.

More than 1 in 10 babies are preterm in Sub-Saharan Africa. That is a daunting number. The reality is when you are in the situation, all you want is for your (very) little person to grow strong without any long-term complications and add just a few more grams so you can hold them without fear of hurting them and /or because of being ashamed of them especially when they are still too small. With increased knowledge and experience, we know what we can do differently or better, but we must remain present as parents and supporters to do what is needed in the present moment.

It is physically, emotionally, socially, spiritually, and often financially taxing as there are extended stays in hospitals, clinics, or with relatives, and church fellowships. It can impact the work situation and return to work; sometimes, you don't know what to expect. There are impacts as a couple and as a family. You might not return to your friendship and family circle for months because you need to protect the compromised immunity of a vulnerable little person born too soon. Perhaps more information and more compassion are required. Possibly our facilities need more resources and training.

Naturally, this experience got us thinking so much more about the medical aspect, prevalence, treatment, and management of this condition. The statistics are grim. Over 1 million children die each year due to complications of prematurity. Many survivors face a lifetime of disability and learning disorders, even visual and hearing impairments.[2] Preterm births are on the increase in almost all countries across the world. Prematurity is the leading cause of newborn deaths; babies die in the first four weeks of life. Global progress in child survival and health in the future cannot be achieved without addressing preterm birth. Governments and action groups, large and small,

---

[2] www.who.int/pmnch/media/news/2012/preterm_birth_report/en/index.html

have brought this item to the development agenda, and we pray that the statistics will reduce soon.

This subject is critical for knowledge generators such as professors, doctors, nurses, midwives, nutritionists, dieticians, counselors, and students in training institutions. For instance, Alex is involved with medical schools and institutions' training in nutrition and dietetics. There are trained medical doctors, nurses, midwives, clinical officers, nutritionists, dietitians, and other professionals who follow the learning curricula suited to the Uganda context.

It is helpful for these practitioners and specialists to understand the actual practicalities of preterm birth, smoothly linking theory to real-life situations. It is the same as the firefighter's or emergency security workers' calculations, formulae, and graphics best come alive through hands-on experience. We were among the fortunate ones with sufficient information, resources, and treatments before, during, and after the pregnancy. Millions worldwide do not even have access to the basics in this regard. We did, however, note that while medical teams are trained in the clinical aspects, they often don't counsel mothers with risk factors for preterm birth. This is perhaps because they're not conversant with the Management of Small and Nutritionally At-Risk Infants under Six Months and Their Mothers (MAMI) care pathway, which aims to provide early treatment to prevent immediate and future poor outcomes, such as more severe or recurrent malnutrition, illness, poor development, and death[3]. Simple actions include empowering them with tools to screen and manage small and nutritionally at-risk mother-infant-pairs consistently.

The statistics tell us that this is a common and dangerous medical condition, and not all the answers exist, but at least two human beings are going through the experience. We hope the information and experiences shared herein motivate doctors, nutritionists, dieticians, midwives, and nursing personnel to increase their support for parents and families in this regard. In Africa, it might be that a family cannot manage the trek to the hospital or clinic every day for months on end, with mothers often being quarantined in the NICU. Thus, the medical teams are the only people they see for weeks and months. The human touch and just understanding could bring some relief.

There are also agencies and regulatory bodies, which include policy-making bodies, such as the Ministry of Health in Uganda. Based on alignment with global sustainable development goals around Zero hunger and good health and well-being, infant and maternal health and nutrition policies have been formulated and documented, but many still need to be implemented. Some regulations are flawed, and

---

[3] MAMI Global Network, ENN, LSHTM (2021). MAMI Care Pathway Package, Version 3 (2021). www.ennonline.net/mamicarepathway

compliance may increase as more experiences (not merely statistics) are shared.

Regarding Labor Laws, maternity leave benefits may need some revision as emergency preterm deliveries will disrupt women's initial workplace agreements. It is not entirely unimaginable that some women may have to take unpaid leave at some point or lose their employment altogether through unforeseen cases. It thus has a socio-economic impact as well. For instance, the Uganda government's Employment Act 2006 doesn't include preterm birth under paid maternity leave for working mothers. The Act provides 60 working days (approximately 12 weeks) of maternity leave for pregnant employees. There are no specific additional provisions in the Employment Act for preterm births.

With millions of cases worldwide each year, thousands of associations, Foundations, NGOs, the UN, donors, and private entities are engaged in child welfare, including preterm births with complications. Our ongoing research in the field can also support information sharing with these organizations, which can ultimately help us reduce the numbers on the continent.

Human beings operate in interdependent systems, and as such, an expecting mother affects and is affected by broader systems such as family, cultural, religious, spiritual, health systems, etc. As we survived our ordeal, we saw society coming to bear on new life in various ways. If we are to decrease maternal and infant mortality, we need to support all societal levels, supporting the practices that work and critically interrogating outdated ones that increase risk. There may be a tendency to misinterpret preterm births or, through misinformation, pressure couples.

We encourage mothers, fathers, and families to remain positive, believing that small changes can bring fantastic results in the long term. In hindsight, one will be tempted to ask many questions, but it is more important to take the lessons and new information and move forward. Regrets and misgivings will sap the energy you need to heal the mind, body, and spirit to welcome your slightly-tinier-than-others bundle of joy and take each day as it comes.

Fathers should be prepared beyond just the preterm baby but also for the spouse who gets scarred from a c-section **how many are ready for such changes and are willing to carry them out? How many are prepared to shoulder blame from in-laws and parents for refusing to take the newborn to them within the culturally dictated timeframe? How many are ready to do kangaroo mother care (KMC), express breastmilk from their spouse, walk into and out of the ICU to feed the baby, etc.?**

We share all the information and best practices we can find so that we reduce the maternal and infant mortality rates on the continent, enhance relationships, and help them on their development path. We will share our story and then share a breakdown of all the tips and tools to make the journey to parenthood as smooth as possible.

❧❧❧❧❧

PART ONE

✎✎✎✎✎

BEFORE THE BIRTH

CHAPTER 1

✤✤✤✤✤

OUR BACKGROUND

We are Stella and Alex Mokori, the proud parents of a Baby Born Too Soon. Our son is now developing well, through grace, much intercession, and medical interventions, bringing us so much joy and laughter that we sometimes forget he was ready to come when his mother had other plans.

Stella was born in 1988 in Nyakishonjwa, Kyeshero, Kayonza, Kanungu District. Born to teachers, she came from a family of eight, the second of three daughters. Unlike our son, she was born at home without any complications. She had a great childhood, and as I got the story, was a bit of a handful as a child, but with a strict headmaster father who prioritized education above all else, she didn't have much wiggle room; she was going to study and make something of her life.

With both parents being teachers, she started school early and enjoyed the experience of good schools (although financial constraints of many siblings studying at the same time meant she did not attend the institutions that invited her) and upon completion of her high school, joined Makerere University which was a whole 560km from home. The distance alone provided abundant evidence that a degree would be completed in one take; there was neither time nor money for retakes, shortcuts, or fooling around. She has one chance to get it done.

She completed a Bachelor of Commerce degree in accounting to the exact timeline. Even before she received her results, she found an assistant accountant position at the International Hospital Kampala. Even though she stayed just under a year, she learned so much about hospitals and their operating models and met many doctors.

She joined the USAID Strengthening Partnerships and Results in Nutrition Globally (SPRING) project in Mbarara as a Finance Assistant in 2012. It was also where we met. She worked herself up in Finance and Administration. Four years into that position, she embarked on her CPA and, in 2016, joined the Research Triangle Institute (RTI) in Kampala. A year later, we were married and started our lives together. The CPA qualification afforded her several exemptions, and she shortly after enrolled for her master's degree with the Cyprus Institute of Marketing. It was not to be all smooth sailing.

The personal and professional growth agenda became hectic; it was work, a new marriage, demanding studies, and involvement in various business ventures, and then I also fell pregnant. She had to complete her master's two months after the birth while things were challenging with the little boy. She has shown the most resilience, but the effects of stress and pressure cannot be overemphasized in the case of preterm pregnancies and delivery. The goal of maintaining a healthy work-life balance and establishing a support relationship as a couple has been a critical learning point. We were inexperienced, and our expectations of each other may have been misaligned.

Stella is so determined that our son has the best of everything that he has the best start she perhaps did not have. She works extra hard so that he doesn't have to face the same struggles she did. She is undoubtedly one of the most determined women I know, so I would watch her formulate a strategy if a goal is to be achieved. She knows what is and what is right, and there is very little chance of her being manipulated to think or act otherwise.

She benefits from robust and committed role models who have supported us and put family above all else. One of her greatest strengths is determination. But, with such a strong work ethic and relentless diligence comes impatience. Stella wants things to happen, preferably without delay. Well, she did, until that fateful call from the gynecologist. A preemie teaches patience, whether virtue or value already possessed or mastered, through sacrifice, prayer, and surrender.

Alex, a professional nutritionist with years of experience in healthcare and nutrition management, established a medical center near our home. That facility played a vital role in our son's recovery and even saved lives the night I needed an emergency operation. Drawing on his deep understanding of maternal and child nutrition, Alex navigated the challenges of fatherhood with a preterm baby. This firsthand knowledge shapes his support for parents, emphasizing the importance of early intervention and proper nutrition for preterm infants.

We attend Makerere Full Gospel Church, and one Sunday during the service, he had a vision and got a name for the baby. He opened the Bible to confirm that this was what we would call our baby. Jair. Alex showed me the name and wrote it down in a book. Later, when we read the meaning, we were enlightened. His name means Provider of the light, and we just felt that he would come to fulfill the meaning of his name. We believe God gave it to us, and at this young age, it already resonates with the kind of person he is. As he grows, we think he will embody what the name implies. But it was a more leisurely start.

All was well in the week to two days following Jair's birth. We were content, often having friends around. We had the little photos, sonars, and scans, enthusiastically documenting the pregnancy in a beautiful photo collection. We used to write stories through letters for him. Each day, we added to the story our great expectations.

But then, mere days before he was born, something went awry. To this day, I still believe it was God's Hand at work because Alex usually returns to Moroto, a town 528 km in Northeastern Uganda, from our marital home in the suburbs of Kampala over the weekend. Still, he worked from their Head Office in Kampala that week. He was meant to travel back on Sunday, so, as fate would have it, on Friday, the car just got stuck in the middle of the road somewhere in Bukoto, a Kampala suburb, as he went to the office.

They tried their best to get the car repaired, and by the time he made it home, all was in good order. But during the night, I started experiencing some difficulties. This prompted me to walk to our medical center, only a few meters from our house, for a checkup by the midwife. The assessment indicated elevated blood pressure, which required urgent medical attention, preferably by a more advanced hospital.

I called Alex (who was having a slight nap) from home, and together with the midwife, we rushed to International Hospital Kampala (IHK), where I had been receiving antenatal care. I was accepted and immediately admitted to the Emergency room for first aid and tests.

Blessedly, the attending doctor in the hospital noted a high-risk blood pressure-related issue, which he recognized from all the antenatal sessions we attended together. After tests and X-rays, they diagnosed the pre-eclampsia and pointed out that the baby was not growing well. The only thing that could save him was an emergency operation, but they first had to stabilize me because of my out-of-range blood pressure. The doctors also wanted the pregnancy to cross over to at least 34 weeks. Two fretful days later, the emergency operation was conducted, and Jair was delivered by C-section. This was certainly not a good experience for us as first-time parents living alone.

Our story is about the miracle and joy of new life but also about sharing the experience with others who have gone through or who will go through a preterm birth. As a Dad, he had a technical advantage as a Nutritionist, and maternal and childcare issues and nutrition are part of his daily role. Alex was with me from the moment I was admitted to the hospital to the point I was wheeled into the operating theatre.

Stella was, and remains, a strong person because I saw others in the hospital in the same situation who were more prominent and probably even more experienced in being devastated. I was in the theatre, and I was the one who received Jair. I remember so vividly being in that theatre, them giving him to me, taking him in my hands, praying with him, dedicating him, and then eventually handing him over to the midwife who brought him into the neonatal nursery.

He was born with a low birth weight of 1.7 kg at 34 weeks.

He was physically strong and well-developed despite being small. And so, to someone having a full-term baby, a preemie can look a bit scary. And I must say even Stella feared him. She couldn't believe what she saw, and it took her some time to get used to it.

But I think the good thing is that we were all by her side and supported her in all ways possible. After the C-section, Stella remained in the ICU as they continued to monitor and stabilize her because of her high blood pressure. The doctors didn't want to let her go to the general ward as her condition was still critical.

It was my responsibility to ensure that Jair got that first breast milk, which we call colostrum. Given his low birth weight, he needed all the essential nutrients from the breast milk, and there are no better sources of nutrients than colostrum and breast milk. So, when I followed him to the nursery, the first thing the midwife told me was to send infant formula because this baby was hungry. I refused and said I would get breast milk from the mother.

She stared at me in disbelief, but I proved I was way more serious than she could imagine. It wasn't always easy getting into the ICU, but I convinced the doctors that the baby was hungry. I remember the first day I went to get the milk from Jair's mother, and people looked at it in disgust. I didn't care what it looked like, how much it was, or what anyone else had to say about it.

The doctors also wanted the pregnancy to cross over to at least 34 weeks. My prayer was for my wife and child to leave the hospital healthy. I continued those milk rounds until Stella was eventually discharged from the ICU and taken to a general ward, and she was able to meet Jair. She was still getting used to having a tiny baby by her side, to whom we had to provide exceptional care.

Friends, relatives, and particularly grandparents shared our joy and awaited our new arrival. We counted the weeks, and we were on track. Until we weren't suddenly got a medical emergency that necessitated his arrival before the expected date.

Our experience has taught us that sometimes things don't go according to our plan despite all our efforts. We learned first-hand that irrespective of status or material comforts, any parent is prone to getting unexpected childbirth results. Therefore, they should be willing and ready to support the mother and infant in overcoming these situations and saving lives. This is vital to understand because more than the trauma of a preterm baby is the prejudice and misinformation associated with it, particularly in Africa.

In our instance, Alex is a medical professional, and Stella is a senior Finance Professional. We enjoyed access to one of the best facilities and could afford all the necessary antenatal care. We had good, experienced midwives and doctors taking care of us. Stella had the best nutrition and practiced effective self-care as best she could despite being involved in multiple endeavors throughout the pregnancy.

There are several organizations in Uganda and across Africa working on reducing the number of maternal and infant deaths related to early-term pregnancies and births. At the East Africa Preterm Birth Initiative (PTBi-EA), the focus is on saving lives. Each year across the world, one million preterm babies die within the first 28 days of life, while over 300,000 women die in childbirth.[4]

As a mother in the throes of coping with a prem delivery and baby, she wondered where it was a rural vs urban situation. She figured that the stressors in the village may differ from those in the cities. Purely perception, of course, but could there be a varied impact between a life of hard manual labor counterbalanced with fewer external challenges like traffic jams, complex personal and work demands, helpers who are more hazardous than helpful, juggling multiple professional and business goals, or did it just come down that unique balance of other factors?

One thing that remained for her, though, was the stress factor. It tends to compound several other or preexisting conditions.

East Africa Preterm Birth Initiative
[4] https://pretermbirtheastafrica.ucsf.edu/

The true story is that we have gone through it, and maybe it will give hope to parents and support networks. I never believed that it would happen to me or when it happened because, having worked in a hospital before for some months, Alex witnessed how mothers would suffer with preterm babies. It was simply astounding.

So, when the obstetrician called saying Jair would be delivered at 34 weeks, my reflexive thought was: *What is this? What does this mean? How will I survive with a preterm infant? Will the child even grow?*

I got so stressed and couldn't understand it for about twenty-four hours.

That was all the time I had to process it, and then through all the education and evidence that the baby had stopped growing, I agreed to proceed. I am rather impatient and generally don't like waiting, but for once, I was willing to wait for my baby to grow full-term.

At that moment, though, I would've done anything for a slow-motion delay, but the message was blindingly clear: if I didn't go to the theatre for a preterm delivery, I might lose the baby and my life, too.

And there I stood thinking about the difficult pregnancy I had suffered all along, to have suffered all that time and then lose the baby? So, I decided to go; there was nothing more I could do at that stage. So, it is not easy to come to terms with that moment. But embraced it; it worked out for us.

Out of curiosity, I did some of my research. There appears to be an increase in preterm births these days, but years ago, husbands embraced pregnancies and were directly more supportive, understanding that it is such a delicate process. But some men today, instead of treating their women well, often directly or indirectly stress them more.

While it's understandable that they frequently engage in multiple tasks to make ends meet, it's essential to make time for their spouses, especially during pregnancy. It becomes a journey of focus and resilience under pressure.

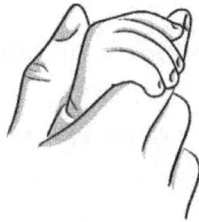

CHAPTER 2

⊷⊷⊷⊷⊷

PREGNANCY PREPARATION

The news of a pregnancy is accepted predominantly with great joy, although sometimes unexpected, as the mother comes to terms with the idea of the baby on its way and the important changes that will no doubt need to be made.

While each pregnancy is unique, and some aspects cannot be fully accounted for, the answer is Yes. Preterm births are an outcome of events that can happen in the womb during the prenatal period, the time when the baby is developing.

One must prepare the environment for the baby, and there are inherent factors to consider, such as a slight build or a preexisting condition such as diabetes. Preparation for pregnancy is best six months before conception. That ensures the body is built enough with the proper nutrients, such as folic acid and iron. Even after conception, good nutrition and exercise are essential. They proactively eliminate factors likely to cause stress and consistently check for complications while offering adequate care and advice.

As an example, multiple births increase the risk factors of a preterm pregnancy. With excessive bleeding and a subsequent iron deficiency, the next pregnancy becomes potentially dangerous.

That is a clear indicator that a medical practitioner can point out to the mother. Still, in other cases, it could be an emergency issue like hypertension, which develops during pregnancy and compounds any number of different symptoms. Factors such as the mother maintaining an ideal weight with sufficient nutrients rather than just letting go of eating anything and everything prompted through hormonal fluctuations. Overweight/obesity is another risk factor for preterm pregnancy and deliveries, so balance and meal plan preparation, where possible, can serve as a preventative measure.

The following sections cover critical considerations and actions to ensure that all bases are covered optimally, preparing to bring new life into the world.

Key factors are vital in the baby's healthy development and the mother's well-being, such as a nutritious diet, proper nutrition, vitamins and minerals, exercise, rest, and avoiding stress during this time.

Nutrition

Expecting a baby is an incomparable experience that women connect with. It creates a new consciousness that even basic things like eating and sleep may need some adjustment.

Eating nutritious meals is one of the best things you can do for your baby's health. Even if eating a healthy diet and exercising weren't very important to you before, now is an excellent time to start implementing healthy habits. Food is medicine. During pregnancy, the mother's diet must be adequate and nutritious. Nutrients first nourish the fetus if she does not consume enough nutrients for herself and the fetus. However, adding 250 calories or two healthy snacks to the daily diet is usually enough to nourish both. Most of the extra calories should be protein.

The diet should be well-balanced or diversified and include fresh fruits, grains, and vegetables. Cereals high in fiber and low in sugar are a good choice. In areas where fish and seafood are available, these are a good option as they contain nutrients that are important for the growth and development of the fetus. However, pregnant women should choose seafood that is low in mercury, and those who are allergic should avoid it altogether.

Stella battled morning sickness from the very start until well up to the fifth month, vomiting and heartburn forcing her in and out of the hospital more times than we care to recall. Keeping anything down was a challenge. At some point, she had faced the little person growing inside her calling shots about what she could eat, when, and how much. Was it not for the grace and understanding of her manager, who knows where her career would be? She felt miserable and disgusted, vomiting and being triggered by every odor and taste. It is only sometimes the case that morning sickness persists that long, and it can be of shorter or longer duration.

What to eat during pregnancy?

Most shops and pharmacies stock prenatal vitamins and supplements to boost mothers and babies, but there are also naturally occurring food sources. In addition to your daily prenatal vitamins and minerals, which will supply you with extra folic acid and iron, you must eat food that balances protein, carbohydrates, calcium, and a wide range of vitamins and minerals available in fruit and vegetables.

Hydration is critical, and it is recommended that mothers drink water regularly throughout the day. Tea and coffee should be replaced with caffeine-free alternatives, and fruit juices should be diluted to avoid excess sugar. A glass of milk each day has also been known to boost the system.

What not to eat or drink during pregnancy

❖ Alcohol

❖ Medication not prescribed or vetted by your doctor or pharmacist must be avoided

❖ Avoid very spicy foods in later months, which can cause heartburn when your stomach is being squeezed upwards by the growing baby.

All the below are possible sources of bacteria that can be harmful to an unborn baby:

❖ Raw seafood

❖ Unpasteurized milk and soft cheese

❖ Undercooked meat and poultry

❖ Leftovers that have not been reheated to steaming hot

How much should pregnant mothers eat?

Eating better doesn't necessarily mean more or overeating. If you start your pregnancy at a healthy weight, you don't need additional calories during the first trimester. In the last six months, you may need slightly more calories to provide your baby with the energy and nourishment necessary. If you're overweight at the start of the pregnancy, the focus should be improving your food choices rather than increasing or decreasing calories. It is not the appropriate time to begin a weight-loss diet in the hopes of not gaining too much pregnancy weight.

Women who begin pregnancy at a healthy weight should ideally gain between 11-16kg by the time they give birth. For women who start their pregnancy overweight, total weight gain should be closer to 7–11kg. Those who are underweight should gain 13–18kg.

Controlling weight gain is harder later in the pregnancy, so the goal is to avoid gaining too much weight during the first few months. However, not gaining enough weight can also cause problems, such as poor fetal growth and labor. Doctors recommend that mothers-to-be add approximately 300 calories to their daily intake to help nourish the developing baby.

Self-Care

Self-care is not only about nutrition; it is about getting rest and taking time to mentally absorb motherhood's reality and imminence. Self-care is about looking after oneself mentally, physically, and emotionally during pregnancy.

Moderate physical activity and exercise are essential for you and the baby; your medical practitioner will guide you. Some research recommends 30 minutes a day. Exercise allows the body to give off feel-good endorphins that can lift the spirit but, in the long term, prepare you for labor and childbirth. It should be moderate; some chores around the home or a walk could be required. Women who have engaged in regular fitness regimes before their pregnancy can continue, perhaps just making a few minor modifications.

Here are a few tips for exercising (and physical tasks) during pregnancy:

Stay cool. Avoid exercising in hot, humid weather as the risk of overheating increases.

Protect your skin. Some form of sunblock is needed for outside exercise because pregnancy increases sensitivity to the sun.

Hydrate. Drink water before, during, and after your workout or activity. Dehydration can contribute to overheating or even trigger contractions, which must be avoided.

Avoid jumping. High-impact jumps are more likely to cause muscle strain and injury because the same pregnancy hormone that helps the uterus expand weakens the body's connective tissues. So, jarring motions and quick directional changes are never a good idea.

It is true that, for some women, pregnancy brings no additional challenges apart from a bit of fatigue and weight gain here and there. They can work until the ninth month, get to the hospital, and have deliveries without complications or slight discomfort. However, in the generality of populations, they are the exception. Most women must make some proactive and extensive changes. Each pregnancy is unique.

Some women have not exercised before pregnancy and might have to start including some mild to moderate activity to gain or improve overall physical and mental well-being. It can be done around the home or in the local community. The following are recommended:

Walking. All it needs is a good pair of supportive shoes (and a sunhat or shade), which can be safely done throughout all nine months of pregnancy.

Swimming is considered the best and safest exercise for pregnant women. It exercises the large muscle groups in both arms and legs, provides cardiovascular benefits, reduces swelling, and makes you feel weightless despite the extra kilos.

Exercise classes for pregnant women can provide slow, controlled exercise, during which an instructor advises on the correct technique to strengthen and tone muscles.

Whether you are a seasoned athlete, enjoy regular exercise, or are just a beginner, listen to your body and don't push yourself beyond your limits. Check-in with your practitioner regularly to ensure you are still safe.

Special Spouse Time

Spending time with your spouse during pregnancy is essential for caring for the baby and mom-to-be.

Even though Stella and I were not always together during the week because of my work commitments, we found exciting ways to prepare for Jair's birth. It is also essential to work on your relationship as a couple, not just as parents, so you don't lose the essence of what brought you together.

Work and study pressures, business demands, hormonal challenges, and energy misalignments may exist, but communication remains critical. It may also be an excellent opportunity to look around the practicalities and find ways to work smarter even around the home.

There is always a better way to get things done or to get rid of things you might no longer need. This creates more time and space for sharing with your spouse, friends, and family. Apart from medical help, love, support, and togetherness make the journey even more significant and, on some days, bearable.

Pregnancy is a great time to be together as a couple and do some things you will probably have less time for in the first few months after the little one arrives.

Sleeping in, watching a movie, going out for a meal or eating at home together, spiritual grounding or worship, and visiting friends and family are just a few ideas for bonding.

Sharing chores or making a short shopping trip together can provide a few moments to connect while getting things done.

Communicate effectively and find ways to make things easy; for example, get more organized around the home or leave notes and diaries of essential stuff so that no one feels left out or forgotten.

Your memories of these times could remind you of the strength of your relationship when you're in the thick of baby care – and sleep-ins are long forgotten.

The middle months of pregnancy are still a long way from birth. This means you and your spouse can think about your hopes and dreams as parents. Parents must decide and agree on how they will parent.

Different backgrounds can make for diverse beliefs and values. This could be the time to share how you see the child coming into the home and what values you will inculcate as parents. Religion, culture, traditions, rituals, and many other aspects could be explored in the months leading up to birth. It will bring up good memories and deepen your couple's connection.

On the other hand, it may bring up unresolved issues involving disparate family roles, such as the involvement of grandparents, the church, or spiritual leaders. This is the time to sort such matters out or at least bring them up for discussion.

There may also be a need to explore financial planning for the child and parents during and after birth. There may now be a need for a full-time helper or nanny, which is an additional expense.

Nesting. In the later stages of pregnancy, parents might want to start building the 'nest' for when the baby or babies arrive. Some even start renovating their homes, looking for a new place to live, beefing up security, or getting a relative to move in with them. This requires discussion and planning.

We photo-documented the pregnancy from the start to share our memories with our little person when the time came so they would know we loved them from the first word. Each day, each of us wrote a heartfelt letter that reminded us of the miracle of life and birth and the impending lifetime responsibility we had lovingly signed up for. With each word, we felt the hand of God in our new role as parents and committed each new day to being the best parents we could be.

Not everyone is lucky enough to have children or a family; we take nothing for granted. It was one of the best ways to connect.

We were very blessed to have each other, but we know this is not always the case for many couples. Not all pregnancies are planned; some occur under unfavorable circumstances. Many spouses deny parenthood and take off at the first word, which may trigger conflict and strife during an already taxing time.

Having the spouse around maybe even less than ideal in instances where there is abuse, violence, substance addiction, and so forth. The mother should seek support and help from trusted or professional sources, remembering that the only priorities are the wellbeing of her and the baby. Other issues are best dealt with afterward in the interest of avoiding any undue stress.

Medical Preparation: Prenatal Care

Prenatal care is health care that a woman gets while pregnant. Going early and regularly for prenatal care can help mothers-to-be and their babies stay healthy. Regular check-ups and care allow doctors to find and deal with problems as early as possible. Best practice suggests that it is vital to start prenatal care as early as possible, even before a woman becomes pregnant.

Sources of Prenatal Care

Pregnant women usually are cared for by:

Obstetricians who are doctors specializing in pregnancy and childbirth

Obstetricians-gynecologists (OB/GYNs): doctors who specialize in pregnancy and childbirth, as well as women's healthcare

Family/General Practitioners: doctors who provide a range of services for patients of all ages (sometimes, this includes obstetrical care) rather than specializing in one area

Certified nurse-midwives: an advanced practice nurse specializing in women's healthcare needs, including prenatal care, labor and delivery, and postpartum care for pregnancies without complications.

Registered Nutritionist/Dietitian (RDN). Play an integral role in prenatal care by providing evidence-based nutritional guidance and support. Their expertise helps ensure the mother and baby receive the nutrients necessary for a healthy pregnancy and optimal development.

Any of these care providers is a good choice if expectant mothers are healthy and there is no reason to expect problems with the pregnancy or delivery.

However, nurse-midwives must have a doctor available for the delivery in case a C-section has to be done.

Your healthcare provider may refer you to a doctor with expertise in high-risk pregnancies if you:

❖ Have a chronic condition like diabetes or heart problems

❖ Have an increased risk of labor

❖ Older than 35 years?

❖ Expecting more than one fetus?

❖ Have other complicated factors that might increase pregnancy risk.

Even if your pregnancy is not high-risk, it may still be an opportune time to change healthcare providers if you're not comfortable with your current doctor.

Routine Visits and Testing

Booking the first checkup during the first 6 - 8 weeks of pregnancy, or a period 2 to 4 weeks later, is advised. Many healthcare providers will only schedule the first visit before eight weeks if there is a problem.

However, WHO recommends that pregnant women have their first contact in the first 12 weeks' gestation, with subsequent contacts taking place at 20, 26, 30, 34, 36, 38, and 40 weeks' gestation.

Specific WHO recommendations include:[5]

❖ A minimum of eight contacts are recommended to reduce perinatal mortality and improve women's care experience.

❖ Counselling about healthy eating and keeping physically active during pregnancy.

❖ Daily oral iron and folic acid supplementation with 30 to 60 mg of elemental iron and 400 µg (0.4 mg) of folic acid for pregnant women to prevent maternal anemia, puerperal sepsis, low birth weight, and preterm birth.

❖ Tetanus toxoid vaccination is recommended for all pregnant women, depending on previous tetanus vaccination exposure, to prevent neonatal mortality from tetanus.

❖ One ultrasound scan before 24 weeks gestation (early ultrasound) is recommended for pregnant women to estimate gestational age, improve detection of fetal anomalies and multiple pregnancies, reduce labor induction for post-term pregnancy, and improve a woman's pregnancy experience.

Health-care providers should ask all pregnant women about their use of alcohol and other

---

[5] WHO recommendations on antenatal care for a positive pregnancy experience. https://iris.who.int/bitstream/handle/10665/250796/9789241549912-eng.pdf?sequence=1.

substances (past and present) as early as possible in the pregnancy and at every antenatal visit.

If mothers are healthy and demonstrate no complicating risk factors, it may be advisable to see the health care provider:

- ❖ Every four weeks until the 28th week of pregnancy

- ❖ Then, every two weeks until 36 weeks

- ❖ Then, once a week until delivery

The mother's weight and blood pressure are usually recorded at each check-up. Starting at the 22nd week, the size and shape of the uterus may also be measured to see whether the fetus is growing and developing normally.

There will also be a urine sample for glucose and protein levels. Glucose screening usually takes place at 12 weeks for women who are at higher risk for gestational diabetes. That includes women who:

- ❖ Previously had a baby that weighed more than 4.1kg

- ❖ Have a family history of diabetes

- ❖ Are obese

All other pregnant women are tested for diabetes at 24- 28 weeks. Mothers are asked to drink a sugary liquid and have blood drawn after an hour for a blood glucose test. If the blood sugar level is high, more testing can confirm whether gestational diabetes is diagnosed.

Prenatal Tests

Depending on the resources available, many parents-to-be opted to have prenatal tests done. These help healthcare providers spot issues such as potential birth defects or chromosomal problems in the fetus. Prenatal tests can be done in the first, second, or third trimesters.

Some prenatal tests are screening tests that can only reveal the possibility of a problem, while diagnostic tests can accurately find the specific situation. A diagnostic test sometimes follows a screening test. These can include blood tests, amniocentesis, and ultrasound exams.

Common Pregnancy Concerns

Some mothers-to-be are concerned about pre-existing medical conditions they already have, such as diabetes, and how it could affect their pregnancy. It's important to talk with your doctor, who may recommend a change in treatment or medication that will reduce any risk.

Other conditions often associated with pregnancy include:[6]

Gestational diabetes: Some pregnant women develop this condition, usually after the first

---

[6] Armando Fuentes, MD, October 2018.

trimester. The placenta provides the fetus with nutrients and oxygen and makes hormones that change how insulin works. Insulin helps the body store sugar in food, which is later converted to energy. In gestational diabetes, a problem with insulin leads to a high blood sugar level.

Preeclampsia: This condition may also be referred to as toxemia of pregnancy. It can happen after the sixth month, causing high blood pressure, edema (fluid buildup in body tissues causing swelling of the hands, feet, or face), and protein in the urine. This is what caused the need for Stella's emergency delivery.

Rh-negative mother/Rh-positive fetus. This is also called Rh incompatibility. Rh incompatibility occurs when a pregnant woman with Rh-negative blood type carries a fetus with Rh-positive blood type. This can lead to complications if the mother's immune system develops antibodies against the fetus's Rh-positive blood cells, treating them as foreign invaders.

Most people have Rh factor in their red blood cells, which means that they are Rh-positive). Those who do not possess it are Rh negative. A simple blood test can determine your Rh factor. If your baby is Rh positive and you're Rh negative, problems can happen when the baby's blood cells enter your bloodstream. Your body may react by making antibodies that can pass into the fetus's bloodstream and destroy red blood cells.

These conditions are severe but manageable. Thus, knowledge helps expectant mothers and spouses to have informed discussions with their healthcare providers.

Some general precautions:

* ❖ Avoid smoking and drugs

* ❖ Avoid over-the-counter medication unless prescribed by your medical practitioner. This includes herbal and natural remedies, supplements, and vitamins. Just because it works for one mom does not guarantee it is safe at any stage of the pregnancy or for all mothers.

Food Safety

During pregnancy, it is also important to avoid foodborne illnesses, such as listeriosis and toxoplasmosis, which can be life-threatening to an unborn baby and may cause birth defects or miscarriage. Foods to steer clear of include:

* ❖ Soft, unpasteurized cheeses

* ❖ Unpasteurized milk, juices, and apple cider

* ❖ Raw eggs or foods containing raw eggs, including Homemade Mayonnaise and Ice Cream

* ❖ Raw or undercooked meats, fish, or shellfish

* ❖ Processed meats

Vaccines

Doctors and specialists must be consulted regarding vaccines during pregnancy. The flu shot can curb flu-related problems for expectant moms, who are at higher risk of problems from the illness. The Centers for Disease Control and Prevention (CDC) recommends using flu shots during any stage of pregnancy.

The Tdap vaccine (against tetanus, diphtheria, and pertussis) is now recommended for all pregnant women in the second half of each pregnancy, regardless of whether they've gotten it before or when it was last given. This is due to the rise in pertussis (whooping cough) infections, which can be fatal in newborns without routine vaccinations.

Physical Changes of Pregnancy

Pregnancy can cause some uncomfortable (not necessarily serious) changes, which could also be discussed with a healthcare practitioner, including:

- ❖ Nausea and vomiting, especially early in the pregnancy
- ❖ Leg swelling and varicose veins
- ❖ Heartburn and constipation
- ❖ Backache
- ❖ Tiredness
- ❖ Loss of sleep
- ❖ Hemorrhoids

❖ Sexual changes

It may be that these conditions feel so strange and new. There may be a tendency to feel too embarrassed or conservative to want to discuss it with the doctor. Still, it is more likely that they have been professionally trained and, in all probability, have heard or seen it all before. The goal is to reduce risk to mother and baby, so use the check-ups to gain as much knowledge and advice as possible.

It is also suggested that a list of questions be kept throughout the pregnancy to identify trends or markers. Mothers must provide the doctor or nurse with as much information as possible, keeping the dialogue open.

Stella advises sticking with the same doctor for the duration of the pregnancy, as they have the history documented and can focus on holistic plans and recommendations.

A doctor must be called immediately in the event of:

❖ Heavy bleeding

❖ A sudden loss of fluid

❖ A noticeable absence of movement by the baby

❖ More than three contractions in an hour

The Stress Factor

Modern life is stressful. Women carry many burdens. Whether they support their families through growing and cooking food and looking after family members or whether they have jobs and careers, a woman's life is stressful. When pregnant, the stress of life takes its toll on the mind and body. The secret is to objectively assess potential stressors within the home, extended family, community, or workplace and address them in ways that promote balance.

One of the significant problems Stella experienced during her pregnancy was mounting stress. Juggling many responsibilities and wanting to do everything well while battling to keep food down and just enough energy to get through the day proved immensely difficult. Urban living and corporate work are stressful in and of themselves, so it was necessary to create balance. With hindsight, it might have been something we could have done better. Stress causes wear and tear on the human body and has disadvantageous long-term effects.

Psycho-social, cultural, and environmental stress triggers experienced during pregnancy can be dangerous, and recent studies suggest that prenatal stress can have consequences that span generations. Prenatal stress can range from *severe* (e.g., trauma from an accident or death notice) to *moderate* (e.g., life event changes such as getting married or moving house) to *mild* (e.g., the experience of daily hassles like traffic jams or insensitive colleagues).

Most human studies show that mild, moderate, and severe stress can negatively influence pregnancy outcomes and the behavioral and physiological development of infants and children. During pregnancy, typical life stress, such as financial or career challenges, may be compounded by worries about the actual pregnancy outcome or the results of prenatal tests and screening. Studies show that both psychosocial stress and pregnancy-specific stresses can have marked effects on pregnancy and human development.

Prenatal stress can indirectly affect infant health and development by increasing the risk of the occurrence of adverse birth outcomes, which are associated with significant developmental and health consequences.

Stress can also activate perinatal depression in mothers, which could negatively affect the mother-infant interaction and/or affect the quality of postnatal care. Prenatal stress can also have direct effects on infant health by altering the course of fetal neurobiological development.

Sometimes, what is needed is to pause from all the hustle and bustle. While pregnancy is not a sickness or disease, a lot happens to the mind and body, even at a cellular level. For some, it feels as if their bodies are being invaded. They are uncomfortable, cannot do things as quickly as they used to, and experience changes in appetite, sleep, sex drive, temperature, blood pressure, etc. And those are not even the psycho-emotional aspects, such as dealing with a spouse, financial stability, and having doubts and fears about pregnancy and parenthood in general. It is a lot and for a long time.

Sometimes, a few moments or days to pause is required. Life gets busy: there may be a career, relationship, family responsibilities, other children, studies, goals, and dreams that exist alongside pregnancy. Life doesn't stop because your morning sickness is so bad; deadlines are not moved because you couldn't get out of bed that morning. In some homes, women are responsible for most of the caregiving, cooking, and chores.

In corporate environments, women often must work twice as hard to prove they deserve to be there, adding another nuance of rush and pressure. Some have helpers, drivers, gardeners, and maintenance teams, and others must be all that, and the dad, too, where relationships have not survived through the pregnancy. All these elements can precipitate stress, which is known to trigger severe complications and even preterm births.

Belief Systems and Pregnancy Preparation

We cannot deny that belief systems, traditions, and customs will impact the pregnancy experience. An interesting study on midwifery in the Bohlabela district in Limpopo, South Africa, highlighted some reasons why many African women do not seek prenatal and antenatal care, often with dire consequences.[7]

It revealed that the indigenous beliefs and practices of expectant women have an influence on their attendance at antenatal clinics. These practices take shape around the cultural traits that are present across generations. It became apparent that the fear of bewitchment is one of the most significant reasons why women are reluctant to get to a hospital or clinic often during the critical early stages. While pregnancy is regarded as sacred, there is a need to maintain secrecy to avoid evil spirits being inflicted on the mother, resulting in malformation of the fetus or worse.

Furthermore, there is more trust in the knowledge of traditional birth attendants, and they prefer their care and expertise to the treatment they receive from midwives in hospitals and clinics who disregard their indigenous beliefs and practices. From this research, it is recommended that Indigenous beliefs and practices be incorporated into the midwifery curriculum so that the health sector can meet the needs of all community members.

The findings were not limited to South Africa; a study by Tsu (1994) in Zimbabwe indicated that most women reported to clinics during the third trimester,

---

[7] Ngomane, S., Mulaudzi, F.M., "Indigenous beliefs and practices that influence the delayed attendance of antenatal clinics by women in the Bohlabela district in Limpopo, South Africa." *Midwifery* (2010), doi: 10.1016/j.midw.2010.11.002.

resulting in adverse birth outcomes. Aspects like religion also impact rituals and practices engaged during pregnancy to preserve safety and health.

Summary

It is critical to understand the holistic nature of pregnancy. It Is not just about a developing fetus. It is a mother's internal and external environment meshing with another new, unknown system, and it can be as daunting as it is exciting. Often, it is downright dangerous, and in our case, it had an impact beyond Jair's birth.

Mothers and caregivers can do many proactive and preventative things to alleviate stress and pressure, invest in the proper diet and exercise, and find the balance between current priorities and all the new changes that come along the way. Some couples are blessed to have all they need to survive the pregnancy. Still, if the statistics are anything to go by, millions of women experience risky and traumatic pregnancies, deliveries, and postnatal conditions.

In continents like Africa and Asia and countries like Australia, there is a misalignment between modern medical practices and traditional or indigenous practices, which often sees mothers delaying seeking medical attention and the eight mandatory check-ups recommended by the World Health Organization.

Each woman and pregnancy are unique, and the physical, mental, emotional, and social resources may differ, so it is essential to stay close to the practitioner but also to listen to one's body and become more in tune, pacing the changes and even documenting the various stages or trimesters.

CHAPTER 3

⤳⤳⤳⤳⤳

WHEN FULL TERM IS NOT AN OPTION

Pregnancy lasts roughly 280 days (40 weeks) on average. A premature or preterm baby is born before the 37th week of pregnancy, according to the World Health Organization. Globally, 15 million infants are born preterm each year, and one million die due to prematurity. Over 60 percent of preterm births occur in Africa and South Asia.

Uganda ranks 28th worldwide in preterm births, with an estimated 13.6 per 1,000 live births. Approximately 226,000 babies are born too soon every year, and of these, 12,500 children under five die due to preterm complications. Many survivors face a lifetime of disability, including learning disabilities and visual and hearing problems. So, it is good to avoid the dangers of early births by informing yourself of them beforehand.

What Causes Preterm Birth?

According to the World Health Organization, preterm birth can occur for various reasons, often happening spontaneously. In some cases, medical reasons such as infections or pregnancy complications necessitate early induction of labor or a cesarean section.

While more research is needed to understand the causes and mechanisms behind preterm birth fully, several factors have been identified. These include multiple pregnancies, infections, and chronic conditions such as diabetes and high blood pressure. However, in many instances, no specific cause is identified. There may also be a genetic influence contributing to preterm births.[8]

Warning Signs

Given the conditions in our country, preterm birth is likely to occur among women living in rural areas and those who do not attend antenatal care (ANC). Living in the capital of Uganda and diligently having attended all our ANC appointments, having had access to the best midwives, obstetricians/gynecologists, and doctors in one of the best private hospitals in Kampala did not spare us from this calamity.

---

[8] *Preterm birth.* 10 May 2023. Key Facts. World Health Organization. www.who.int/news-room/fact-sheets/ detail/ preterm-birth.

Before Jair was born, all was well. We were happy to spend most of our time documenting daily pictorial stories of the pregnancy for our baby to find after birth. We journaled stories for him so we could read them to him once he was born. Also, friends often came around to check on the progress of the pregnancy and Stella's condition. However, just days before he was born, she had an uneasy experience.

Up to now, I still believe that God was at work because I usually went back to my then-duty station in Moroto in Northeastern Uganda over the weekend. Still, I worked from our Head Office in Kampala that week, waiting to travel back to Moroto that Sunday.

So, as fate would have it, the red flags all started with our car getting spoilt in the middle of the road, somewhere in Bukoto, one of the suburbs in Kampala, on a Friday as I went to work. I did everything to ensure that the car was repaired immediately, knowing that we needed it in good shape any day now. Little did I know that that night was the long-awaited moment, although it came too soon.

Preeclampsia

During that very night, my wife started experiencing severe discomfort suddenly. One thing that we all found so helpful at that moment was Lynwood Medical Center, which we opened near our home, whose midwife provided us with the diagnosis that Stella had developed Preeclampsia. The midwife also administered first aid to stabilize Stella. To our shock, we never saw this condition coming, and neither did any of her doctors see signs of it during any of her antenatal visits.

Preeclampsia is a pregnancy complication characterized by high blood pressure and signs of damage to another organ system, most often the liver and kidneys. Preeclampsia usually begins after 20 weeks of pregnancy in women whose blood pressure has been normal.

Upon getting the news of this condition and its danger to both the baby and mother, we had to rush to the hospital; otherwise, if we had delayed, things would have been worse. The midwife at our Medical Center escorted us to the hospital. Upon getting into the hospital, tests were done, and X-rays were taken.

Usually, abdominal X-rays during pregnancy are rarely taken. Still, sometimes, because of a particular medical condition, your physician may feel that a diagnostic X-ray of your abdomen or lower torso is needed, just like in our case.

Eventually, all the test results attested that there was preeclampsia and the baby was not growing well. And the only thing that needed to be done to save him was to have an emergency Cesarean section.

Many doctors prefer to perform caesareans for women with severe pre-eclampsia, even when the baby is healthy. Nevertheless, observational studies have demonstrated that cesarean section may worsen the outlook for mother and baby, with an increased risk of complications. So, with this knowledge, the mother had to be stabilized first because her blood pressure was too high.

The obstetrician also wanted the baby to cross over to 34 weeks. She was put on medication to control high blood pressure and to help the baby's lungs mature. So, after two days, the emergency operation was over, and there was Jair. We had mixed feelings being first-time parents. That was not an expected experience, although we were happy he was finally here and still grateful to God for how he came to us.

What Did Our Preterm Baby Look Like?

I was by my wife's side from when she was admitted into the hospital to the point when she got into the theatre for that operation, and I am the one who gladly received Jair.

I remember the midwife and the surgeon handing him over to me, getting him in my hands, praying with him, dedicating him, and then eventually handing him over to the midwife, who later took him into the Neonatal Intensive Care Unit (NICU). Jair was born weighing 1.7 KG at 34 weeks.

A Baby Born at 34 Weeks

What is the typical size, weight, and physical appearance of a baby born at 34 weeks?

On average, a baby born at 34 weeks weighs about 5.2 pounds (2,377 grams) and is about 17.8 inches (45.6 centimeters) long. Preemies may look thin and fragile compared to full-term babies, and their stomachs and heads may appear oversized for their small limbs. These babies' skins may look shiny, transparent, dry, or flaky since there may not be enough fat beneath their skin to keep the infant warm as it's premature. Very premature newborns' eyes may be welded shut at first.

However, they ought to be able to respond to varied sights by 30 weeks. On the other hand, some babies' eyes can be injured by aberrant blood vessel growth in the retina. Preterm babies and babies given too much oxygen are more likely to have this problem. This can lead to vision loss or even complete blindness. Immature development could also cause a baby to be unable to control his or her body temperature, respiration, or heart rate. They may twitch, stiffen, limp, or lose their ability to stay attentive.

Despite all the above facts about preemies, our baby was mature, robust, and looking great, so much so that having a baby who looked mature with such an enormous weight was a bit scary. And I must say even the mother was scared. She couldn't believe what she was seeing, and it took her some time to get used to what Jair looked like and weighed.

Preterm Babies May Suffer Some Problems

Preterm babies are more likely to acquire health impairments that can last their entire lives. How much this will impact their life depends on how soon they were born, the quality of care they received during and after birth, and the days and weeks that followed.

While outcomes have improved for preterm babies, given all the available medical technology, complications can still occur. The following complications can affect preterm babies in the first weeks after birth.

Gastrointestinal Problems

This is the most common and serious intestinal disease among preterm babies. It happens when small or large intestine tissue is injured or inflamed. An undeveloped gastrointestinal system, too little oxygen or blood flow to the intestine at birth or later, a viral or bacterial infection of the intestine, and formula feeding all lead to issues like necrotizing enterocolitis or NEC.

Brain Problems

Preterm birth can lead to long-term intellectual and developmental disabilities for babies. These are problems with how the brain works. They can cause a person to have trouble or delays in physical development, learning, communicating, taking care of himself, and getting along with others.

Some long-term conditions linked to preterm birth include:

Cerebral palsy (also called CP). This group of conditions affects the parts of your brain that control your muscles. This can cause problems with movement, posture (standing up straight), and balance.

Behavior problems. Some studies show that preterm babies may be more likely to have attention deficit hyperactivity disorder (also called ADHD) than babies born on time. ADHD is a condition that makes it hard for a person to pay attention and control his behavior.

Mental health conditions. Preterm babies may be more likely to have anxiety or depression later in life. Depression is a medical condition in which strong feelings of sadness last for a long time and interfere with your daily life. It needs treatment to get better. Anxiety is when you feel worried or fearful; these feelings affect your daily life, like schoolwork, jobs, or relationships.

Neurological disorders. These conditions affect the body's brain, spinal cord, and nerves.

The chances of intraventricular hemorrhage (IVH) of the newborn bleeding into the fluid-filled areas, or ventricles, surrounded by the brain increase the earlier a baby is born, and the smaller and more preterm the infant, the higher the risk for IVH. Most hemorrhages are minor and have a minimal long-term impact.

Heart Problems

In preterm babies, one of the most common heart problems is Patent ductus arteriosus (PDA). When babies are in the womb, their blood gets oxygen from the placenta. Their lungs don't work until the umbilical cord is cut after birth. Before birth, a blood vessel called the ductus arteriosus diverts blood from the lungs. This blood vessel closes a few days after birth. In preterm babies, it's common for this closure to be delayed. This is known as patent ductus arteriosus (PDA).

Congenital Heart Disease (CHD) is another heart problem in preemies. The medical term 'congenital heart disease' describes a range of heart problems that affect how the heart works. They happen when the heart doesn't develop properly in the womb.

An ultrasound scan usually diagnoses it, called an echocardiogram (sometimes called 'echo' for short).

Some types of CHD, such as small holes in the heart, don't need treatment if they're likely to improve independently.

Other heart problems are more severe and need treatment. Surgery isn't always possible or safe for very premature babies. If your baby is too tiny for surgery, the healthcare team will delay treatment to give your baby time to grow and develop.

Low blood pressure (hypotension) is quite common in preterm babies and doesn't always need treatment. If your baby's blood pressure falls too low and they have blood circulation problems, they need treatment to increase the blood flow to their organs. Low blood pressure can necessitate the usage of intravenous fluids, medications, and blood transfusions.

Breathing Problems

A preterm baby may have difficulty breathing due to an undeveloped respiratory system. Newborn respiratory distress syndrome (NRDS) occurs when a baby's lungs are not fully developed and cannot provide enough oxygen, causing breathing difficulties.

It is also known as infant respiratory distress syndrome, hyaline membrane disease, or surfactant deficiency lung disease. As a result, the baby may suffer from minor issues later in life. For example, the development of sinuses, lungs leak air into the chest, the sac around the heart, or elsewhere in the chest, and chronic lung disease (bronchopulmonary dysplasia).

Similarly, babies can get congested when they breathe in even a bit of cigarette smoke, pollutants, viruses, and other irritants. Their bodies aren't yet able to produce extra mucus in the nose and airways to trap and remove these irritants.

Blood Problems

Blood disorders, such as anemia and infant jaundice, can occur in preterm babies due to their lower number of red blood cells (RBC). These RBCs also have a shorter life span than the red blood cells of full-term babies. This is called anemia of prematurity. While all newborns experience a steady decrease in red blood cell count over the first few months of life, preterm babies may experience a faster drop.

Prematurity anemia is caused by untimely birth occurring before placental iron transport; fetal erythropoiesis is complete, phlebotomy blood losses taken for laboratory testing, low plasma levels of erythropoietin due to diminished production and accelerated catabolism, rapid body growth and the need for a commensurate increase in red cell volume/mass, and disorders causing RBC losses due to bleeding and hemolysis.

Delayed Language Development

Most preterm babies develop language skills, but their development may be delayed. Compared to full-term children, they might need help speaking and understanding what's said to them. Language problems can also sometimes be an early sign of hearing, thinking, or learning problems.

Preterm babies are also at risk of delays in motor skills, the integration of primitive reflexes, and cognition development, all of which can impact language development.

A speech therapist can help provide the child with the best support possible to ensure an optimal language learning environment. This will involve working directly with the child and doing parent training. Intervention for language delays in preterm children is the same as one used for general language delays; the difference is often the over-sight and insufficient monitoring for children at risk.

Early intervention with the help of a speech-language pathologist is critical as the brain develops and matures and forms new neural pathways, especially before age 3. Speech therapy would target cognitive, language, speech, and social communication abilities. A Speech Therapist would also watch for broader symptoms requiring referrals to other specialized professionals.

In Uganda, preterm birth complications alone contribute 38 percent of all deaths of babies younger than one month of age. This is the situation even when we know what can be done to prevent many of these deaths. One of the highest-impact interventions for newborn survival and health is kangaroo mother care (KMC). Kangaroo care is when you lay your diapered baby on your bare chest (if you're the father) or between your bare breasts (if you're the mother). It's also called skin-to-skin care because your baby's bare skin is touching your bare skin. Put a blanket on your baby's back to help keep him warm.

I, the mother, provided KMC to Jair right from the hospital to our home for months. Whereas the mother was still in the ICU and later in the ward for recovery, I provided KMC for him. We were in and out of the hospital for a month after the mother recovered.

So, I went in to care for our baby, which wasn't easy because imagine kangarooing the child when you're tired. I was still getting used to the fact that I had a tiny baby by my side that I had to provide KMC for him to not only bond but to help regulate his heart rate and breathing, calm him, give him better sleep, promote brain development, boost his immune system and reduce crying. I can attest that this exercise performed miracles for our baby and helped us reduce his chances of being affected by the health problems faced by babies of his kind.

Medical Reasons Why Some Babies Are Born Early

Preterm birth is sometimes planned because it is safer for the mother and the infant. This could be due to a medical problem affecting the mother or the child. You may be offered an induction or a cesarean procedure if you are recommended to give earlier birth.

However, natural preterm births usually happen on their own; they can be harmful to both the baby and the mother.

Many circumstances can cause preterm birth. Women who have already had a preterm baby and those who are pregnant with twins or triplets or have uterine or cervical tumors are at an increased risk. Some other considerations include:

Smoking

Tobacco usage of any form increases a mother's chance of preterm Premature Rupture of the Membranes (PPROM) and preterm labor. Nicotine constricts blood arteries in the uterus, preventing nutrients and oxygen from reaching the fetus and contributing to early labor.

Your Pregnancy History

If you have already given birth early, you are more likely to do so again. The more preterm deliveries you've had, the higher your risk is.

Genetics

If your mother or sister went into labor early, or if you have had a prior preterm baby, you're more likely to deliver early. Doctors aren't sure why, but being African American boosts a woman's chances of giving birth prematurely.

Polyhydramnios

The fluid that surrounds your baby in the womb is called amniotic fluid. When there is too much amniotic fluid around the fetus during pregnancy, it is called polyhydramnios. This raises the chance of pregnancy problems, such as preterm birth, by a small margin.

Stress

Stress can affect your immune system, which protects you from sickness, whether it is acute or long-term. This increases your chances of getting a uterine infection and has the potential to cause an early birth. Pregnancy may be an extremely emotional time, and it can be difficult to tell if your feelings are normal or whether they are an indication of something more serious.

Uterine Abnormalities

A uterine anomaly occurs when the womb (uterus) forms irregularly before birth. Depending on the form of the womb, preterm birth may be more likely. When most women become pregnant, they are not aware of whether they have an unusually shaped womb or a "normal" one.

Diabetes

Blood sugar levels that are too high might create difficulties during pregnancy and have the potential to harm blood vessels and nerves. They might also cause birth abnormalities in a developing infant due to weakened blood vessels. Blood sugar control before and during pregnancy can help lower the risk of gestational diabetes.

Bleeding After 24 Weeks

Bleeding during the first trimester may indicate a placental issue, such as a low-lying placenta or placental abruption, both of which can result in preterm birth. Even if you have no other symptoms, any bleeding during pregnancy should be checked.

In addition to those stated above, other circumstances and factors may also contribute to preterm birth, and your age may be a factor.

Preterm birth is more likely if you become pregnant before the age of 18 or after the age of 40. Although preterm birth is truly a global problem, most preterm births occur in southern Asia and sub-Saharan Africa. According to statistics, African American women are three times more likely than women of other ethnicities to give birth prematurely.

Preterm birth is also more likely in women who are not at a healthy weight (over or underweight) when they get pregnant.

Coping With an Early Arrival

Having a child is likely to be one of the most life-changing experiences you will ever have. Pregnancy can be stressful enough, but what if you find out your baby is coming too soon? This can be a challenging thing to deal with mentally, emotionally, physically, and spiritually.

A specific expected delivery date (EDD) was given to us throughout the antenatal visits, and everything changed within the blink of an eye. The mental and emotional turmoil caused by this news cannot be dismissed.

We sought explanations from our midwives, nurses, and doctors. They all tried to make us feel as relaxed as possible. To keep the mother's anxiety levels as low as possible, we not only needed to save her life but the baby as well. After the birth, our infant was admitted to the neonatal intensive care unit (NICU). Babies in NICUs are surrounded by a lot of machinery and technology, which can be overwhelming and even frightening at first. It's sometimes difficult to picture the NICU as your child's nursery, but that's precisely what it is.

This can also happen to any mother, just like it did to me. Even after the operation, they couldn't contain me in the regular patients' ward. I had to be transferred to the ICU because I was still in much pain, and my blood pressure was still so high. I stabilized after two weeks.

Dealing with Feelings

A preterm birth, like any birth, involves many emotions. Your emotions might fluctuate from shock to grief, sadness to hope, panic to guilt, and anger to love and joy. However, any positive feelings can be easily masked by fear and concern for your baby.

I would describe the journey of preterm labor and subsequent birth as a roller coaster ride. Regardless, roller coaster rides always come to an end, and through love and support, your ride can have a positive result, just like mine did.

A preterm birth can shake your confidence in the world. It's normal to feel many mixed and sometimes conflicting emotions not only about yourself but others too. I remember feeling so alone and uncared for by my husband while I was pregnant, and yet part of me also understood that he had no idea of what I was going through. And after having the baby, everyone I'd tell the story would feel sorry and ask how I'm managing. Comments about how tiny and dark my baby was would make me feel so bad, but they didn't know that he was a preemie. I decided to keep the story to myself and keep the baby out of sight for the first three months after his birth.

There are positive emotions, of course, like joy and love for your newborn. In my case, I was terrified of even holding him as he was so small, and I couldn't believe that we both had made it through all the pain and trauma. It took me a while to accept Jair's state, especially his physical appearance. I had an opportunity to stay in the hospital with him as I was also being monitored, so the feeling that some moms get when they must leave the hospital without their babies is that separation can bring worse feelings.

However, amidst all this, as a mother, you have no control over what is happening and how you're feeling; you're completely helpless, especially when you're a first-time mother like me. There's nothing you can do to make a difference. To feel powerless is so painful, suspended in time and space, but here's what you can do.

- ❖ Accept your feelings, whatever they are; don't try to suppress them. Acknowledging your emotions at any stage of this journey is a good idea.

- ❖ Tell someone what you are going through. This might be your spouse, a close family member or acquaintance, or a trained professional such as a therapist.

- ❖ If your spouse's coping style differs from yours, accept it.

- ❖ Tell or share your story like we are doing now. It brings healing to the mind, body, and soul, teaches another mother or family member what to do, and reminds them that they aren't alone on their journey.

Looking After a Preemie Baby and Mother

I'm blessed to be a professional nutritionist. I work on maternal childcare and nutrition issues almost every day at work and in my private life.

My wife having been taken to the ICU immediately after having Jair, it was my responsibility to see to it that he gets that first breast milk, which we call colostrum because I knew that given the fact that he was a low birth weight, he needed all the breast milk nutrients possible. There's no better nutrient than that. From the theater, I followed him to the nursery; the midwife first told me to send infant formula because the baby was hungry.

No, I said to the midwife. I am not sending any infant formula. I am going to pump breast milk from the mother. The midwife looked at me in disbelief, wondering if I was serious, but I proved to her that I was more serious than she thought. So, I went to the ICU at that moment. It was difficult to access, but I told the doctors I needed to get colostrum because the baby was hungry. I remember the first time of extraction; the process looked a bit disgusting, and that subjected me to unnecessary attention.

Think about it: my wife was not stable, and here I am expressing food for the baby from her. Given her condition, I managed to get very little colostrum compared to the hunger of the baby. I took it and told the midwife to give it to him. So, I continued making these rounds until the mother was discharged from the ICU and taken to the private ward, where she was now able to meet and introduce suckling to the baby.

Rejecting preemie baby formula at that stage was a difficult but selfless decision, one of the most important I'd ever make for both the mother and baby. I am certain the situation would have been different if I wasn't there. My presence in the hospital ensured my wife, the mother of our baby, had the support she needed to make the right food choice—breast milk, the only choice.

Breast Milk

If your child is having trouble feeding and drinking enough milk, your midwife or neonatal nurse can assist you in using a breast pump or hand-expressing breastmilk for your baby until they are ready to feed on their own.

Your baby will give you indicators that it is ready to breastfeed. As it grows older, its ability to suckle breast milk will improve.

Mother

In addition, some general practices should be practiced at every stage of life.

Eat a diet from a diverse range of sources. Families should aim to provide children with food from four or more food groups each day and eat a range of healthy foods throughout the week.

Animal-sourced foods include chicken, fish, liver, eggs, and milk products. (Note: animal-sourced foods should be started at six months).

Staples: Grains such as maize, rice millet, and sorghum; roots and tubers such as cassava and potatoes.

Legumes such as beans, lentils, peas, and groundnuts; seeds such as sesame.

Fruits and vegetables rich in vitamin A, such as mango, papaya, passion fruit, oranges, dark-green leaves, carrots, sweet potato, and pumpkin; and other fruits and vegetables, such as banana, pineapple, watermelon, tomatoes, avocado, eggplant, and cabbage.

Oil and fats, such as oil seeds, margarine, ghee, and butter, added to vegetables and other foods will improve the absorption of some vitamins and provide extra energy. Infants need only a minimal amount (no more than half a teaspoon daily).

Practice appropriate hygiene, such as using latrines, keeping food and water containers clean, and washing hands before eating or preparing meals.

Prevent and seek treatment for infections early

Every expecting mother needs to eat nutritious foods, engage in physical activity, get as much rest as possible, and devote time to activities you enjoy. Limiting coffee, alcohol, and other substances is also a good idea. Surround yourself with individuals who encourage you to move on and be happy.

Jair's mother always had a poor appetite and did not like eating fruits and vegetables. When she conceived, I had to slowly but continuously help her learn to eat more nutritious foods, including fruits and vegetables. For the sake of the baby, she adjusted. She loved watermelon, pineapple, and other locally available fruits and vegetables. It became almost standard for her to include these in every meal.

After the birth of Jair, I had to focus on helping her eat a diverse diet with all the food groups and an additional two meals to ensure she had enough breast milk for him and that she was energetic enough to carry on with all the other aspects of life.

To support milk production, I got her local vegetables, especially the relatively bitter spider plant (jobbyo), which she ate at least twice daily. I also bought lots of tamarind from Eastern Uganda, which she could put in millet porridge and fruit juices. She did not find any challenges eating these healthy meals as she could do anything for the baby's sake and her health.

Early Labor

Some mothers go into labor early without being informed that their babies will not make it to term. This can be a shocking and frightening experience.

Let's look at some of the early indicators of labor:

You may feel different for up to a week before labor begins. This is because your body is changing as it prepares for birth. You must go to the hospital after speaking with your midwife or doctor.

Staff at the hospital will examine your womb's neck (cervix) to see if it is shortening and opening, indicating that labor has begun. They may conduct an infection test as well.

The hospital may also test for a chemical called "fetal fibronectin" in the fluid in the vaginal canal. The existence of this substance may aid your doctor in determining whether you will carry your baby to term or not.

If it is unclear whether you're in labor or have complications, the doctor will send you to the prenatal ward for monitoring.

The doctor will also want to monitor your baby's heartbeat, which can be done with a monitor strapped to your stomach (a CTG cardiotocography machine).

The hospital can offer you medicine to slow down your labor if you are less than 34 weeks pregnant. This may cause the birth to be postponed long enough for you to be transferred to a hospital that has a neonatal intensive care unit (NICU).

This was the case with us, in which the doctors delayed the delivery by Cesarean section by two days until the pregnancy reached 34 weeks. If you are over 34 weeks pregnant, your doctor will likely let labor progress at its rate. Even though your baby will be tiny, it is likely to do exceptionally well.

The hospital will give you steroid injections to aid in developing your baby's lungs and alleviate breathing problems after birth. This assistance is required because a baby is not entirely ready to breathe air until around 36 weeks of pregnancy.

You don't have to have a cesarean section just because you're in early labor. However, if you are bleeding or your baby is upset, you may require one.

Thinking About Pregnancy After Preterm Birth

If you have had a preterm birth previously (before 37 weeks), you're more likely to have one again. Talk to your doctor about what you can do before and during pregnancy to lower your chances of having a baby too soon.

Waiting at least eighteen months after giving birth before trying to conceive again may reduce your chances of having a preterm baby in your future pregnancy.

A risk factor is something that increases the likelihood of something else happening. Some risk factors are unavoidable, such as having given birth prematurely in a previous pregnancy. Other risk factors are things that you can control.

Being as healthy as possible will help you have a healthy, full-term pregnancy when you are pregnant. Examples are maintaining a healthy weight, getting treatment for health concerns, preventing and treating infections, and decreasing or managing stress.

How Can Preterm Births Be Prevented?

Preterm births are a leading cause of neonatal mortality and account for 35 percent of all neonatal deaths worldwide. Uganda's high preterm birth rate of 13.6 per 1000 live births ranks 28th in the world.

The issue of preterm birth is an outcome of events that can happen in the womb during the prenatal period, that is, the time when the baby is developing.

As nutritionists, we talk about preparing for pregnancy about six months before conception. And that helps to ensure that the body is built well enough, say with the proper nutrients such as folic acid and iron. So, even after conception, we continue to eat well, exercise, eliminate factors likely to cause stress, and, above all, check for any complications that could develop along the way. That also means keeping healthy in terms of preventing disease. It can be in a boot of Malaria; it can be a boot of any infection that can disturb the proper fetal development.

Beyond nutrition in preparation for pregnancy, women and their spouses need to work closely with their doctors and nutritionists to understand the risk factors for preterm birth and otherwise birth outcomes such as low birth weight. This should be taken seriously because pregnancy presents an opportunity to break the generational cycle of malnutrition.

For instance, babies whose mothers are underweight or were stunted as children are more likely to have low birth weight and/or be preterm. Such women are often too short, with smaller bodies and pelvic bones, and experience difficulties in carrying the baby to term or in providing adequate nutrients to have them develop optimally in utero. These women, their spouses, and family members can follow the recommendations below to offset the risks of undernutrition during pregnancy:

- ❖ Visiting a family planning center to discuss which family planning methods are available and most appropriate for the individual's situation. (Using a family planning method is essential to space births adequately.)

- ❖ Ensuring eight health system antenatal contacts. Antenatal care is a critical opportunity for health providers to deliver care, support, and information to pregnant women.

- ❖ Increasing food intake during pregnancy and breastfeeding. During pregnancy, this means eating one extra meal or "snack" (food between meals) each day; during breastfeeding, it means eating two extra meals or "snacks" each day.

- ❖ Take iron/folate supplements (or other recommended supplements for pregnant women) as soon as she knows she is pregnant and continue for at least three months after delivery of the child, according to national recommendations.

* Deworming and giving antimalarial drugs to pregnant women at four or more months of pregnancy.

* Prevention, education, and testing for sexually transmitted infections (STIs), including HIV.

* Letting other family members help with the pregnant woman's workload.

* Resting more, especially during late pregnancy.

* Although it is traditionally not an African culture, husbands/spouses can help break the cycle of malnutrition during pregnancy and lactation:

* Provide extra food for their wives/spouses during pregnancy and lactation.

* Help with household chores to reduce wives'/spouse's workload.

* Encourage their wives/ spouses to deliver the baby to a health facility.

* Plan for safe transportation to the facility (if needed) for birth.

* Encourage their wives/spouses to breastfeed immediately after birth and to continue to

breastfeed, even considering other household, office, and farm responsibilities

❖ Discuss options for family planning together with their wives/ spouses.

❖ Encourage equal access to education for girls and boys.

❖ Accompany their wives in antenatal care and remind them to take their iron/folate tablets.

So, antenatal care must be taken seriously by ensuring that those responsible for the mother's welfare play their part. When medical practitioners also do their due diligence, we can quickly curb this situation.

In rural Uganda, severe household food insecurity, adolescent pregnancy, inadequate birth spacing, malaria infection, suboptimal ANC attendance, and home delivery represent modifiable risk factors associated with higher rates of preterm births. The government and other nongovernmental organizations are trying to see that they establish neonatal intensive care units in national and regional referral hospitals and general hospitals.

This implies that the midwives will be able to identify risky pregnancies in time such that a specialist delivers the mothers and continues to give adequate care and advice; for instance, if a mother doesn't have enough iron and is pregnant, that can become a risk factor.

Preterm birth can be prevented, but in case it comes as an emergency, for instance, due to high blood pressure that develops during pregnancy or excessive weight gain by a mother during pregnancy, visit your doctor for a solution to save both the baby and mother.

Another important thing is to see your doctor early and regularly in your pregnancy for prenatal care. Take care of any health problems, like diabetes, high blood pressure, or depression. Don't smoke, drink, or use illegal drugs. Eat a diet that includes a variety of healthy foods, and drink lots of pure and clean water each day. Uganda is blessed with many nutritious, locally available foods, including fresh vegetables and fruits, which can be eaten at least thrice a day. We often encourage pregnant women to have an additional meal or "snack" (food between meals) for breakfast, lunch, and supper.

More and more babies are surviving despite being born early and being very little, thanks to incredible breakthroughs in the care of ill and preterm babies. On the other hand, early birth prevention is the best approach to ensure that babies have a healthy start in life.

PART TWO

❧❧❧❧❧

YOUR BABY'S BIRTH

CHAPTER 4

ᵅᵅᵅᵅᵅ

CESAREAN VS. NATURAL BIRTH: THE MYTHS VS. THE FACTS

When it comes to childbirth, we all want the same thing: The baby to come out alive! However, the time when the baby comes out can be determined by several factors. It may be a personal decision, while it may be a medical need at other times.

Most women expect a natural birth when they start their pregnancies. Suppose you are pregnant and trying to decide whether natural birth or cesarean delivery is best for you. In that case, there are some significant factors to consider and questions to ask your physician.

What's Cesarean Birth?

In a cesarean birth, the doctor cuts an incision in the abdomen and womb to deliver the baby. In the United

States, about 1 in 3 American babies are born via cesarean. The prevalence of Cesarean section (C-section) delivery in Africa varies by country and region, ranging from 4.9 percent in sub-Saharan Africa to 24.5 percent in South Africa[9]. Cesarean delivery rates increased both at facility and population levels in Uganda. Overall, the CS rate for live births at facilities was 9.9 percent, rising from 8.5 percent in 2012 to 11 percent in 2016. The overall population-based CS rate was 4.7 percent and increased from 3.2 to 5.9 percent over the same period.[10]

Cesarean vs. Natural Birth

The benefits and drawbacks of a cesarean section versus a vaginal delivery are still being debated. In this chapter, we shall examine the advantages and disadvantages of both natural and cesarean births from a medical and well-being standpoint.

---

[9] Md. Akhtarul Islam, Nusrat Jahan Sathi, Md. Tanvir Hossain, Abdul Jabbar, Andre M. N. Renzaho & Sheikh Mohammed Shariful Islam. Caesarean delivery and its association with educational attainment, wealth index, and place of residence in Sub-Saharan Africa: a meta-analysis. *Cientific Reports*, vol. 12, Article number: 5554 (2022). www.nature.com/articles/s41598-022-09567-1#:~:text=Betran%20et%20al.%20reported%20a,%2C%20Sahara n%20Africa%20(3.5%25).

[10] Atuheire et al. Spatial and temporal trends of cesarean deliveries in Uganda: 2012–2016. *BMC Pregnancy and Childbirth* (2019) 19:132. https://bmcpregnancychildbirth.biomedcentral. com/track/pdf/10.1186/s12884-019-2279-6.pdf.

Natural Birth

A vaginal delivery, with or without pain medicine or other medical intervention, is referred to as a "natural birth." The mother oversees her body during a natural delivery, with a midwife or nurse/other healthcare provider gently guiding and supporting her through the labor stages.

Early, active, and transitional labor are the three stages you can expect to go through (or first, second, and third) while giving birth. A doctor or nurse will examine you regularly to evaluate your progress in the phases, including measuring your cervix.

When you reach 10 cm, you are fully dilated, and it is time to push. As you push and the baby progresses through the birth canal, the doctors and midwives will be there to help. Minor contractions will continue as you get ready to deliver the placenta after the baby crowns are delivered.

Pros of Natural Birth

Compared to C-sections, vaginal births usually result in shorter hospital stays and recuperation times. The average period of a hospital stay following a vaginal delivery is one to two days, depending on the laws.

Since major surgery is not required, the mother can start nursing early.

The muscles involved in a vaginal delivery are likely to press out the fluid into the newborn's lungs. This makes it easier for the infant to breathe.

Cons of Natural Birth

Delivering a baby naturally is a long and physically demanding process. First-time mothers often spend four to eight hours in active labor. This is when their cervix is fully dilated, and they are having active and frequent contractions, which can be excruciating at times.

Tissues and skin surrounding the vagina may stretch and tear during an expected delivery when the infant is passing through the birth canal. Sutures may be required in cases of severe tears and strains. Stretching and tearing can cause the pelvic muscles that control urine and bowel movements to become weak or injured.

After a natural birth, discomfort in the perineum (the region between the anus and vagina) may persist.

If a mother's baby is large (bigger than 8 pounds, 13 ounces), the infant may be harmed during the vaginal birth process, resulting in injuries such as a bruised scalp.

As previously stated, having a baby naturally can be unpleasant; therefore, we will discuss techniques for preparing for this significant step.

Prepare Yourself Physically

It is just as crucial to prepare your body as it is to prepare your thoughts for a natural birth. As your body creates a placenta and a baby, adds fluid, and prepares for future breastfeeding, it will undergo dramatic changes. Small, regular, high-protein meals with plenty of fresh vegetables are recommended. Limit processed foods like white flour, sugars, chemical sweeteners, packaged fruits, and drink plenty of water.

Get As Much Exercise as Possible!

It is not about losing weight when you are pregnant; it is about improving your mental health and preparing your body for birth.

Find A Care Provider with Whom You Are Comfortable

According to research, the quality of a woman's relationship with her provider is the most crucial element in determining her satisfaction with her birth experience, regardless of the outcome.

Prepare Your Thoughts

Preparing your mind and soul for natural birth is just as crucial as performing squats for women who wish to give birth naturally. Get a great night's sleep. As your due date approaches, take a nap. Hypo-birthing seminars, audio programs, prenatal meditations, and many books and podcasts are all available to help you learn and relax while pregnant. Meditating and building a profound state of relaxation that you can easily access during stressful situations is critical. You should also mentally prepare yourself by reading pleasant labor stories.

You only have one chance to give birth to your child, so prepare your mind, body, and spirit for the most natural, transforming, and powerful labor possible.

C-Section

The cesarean section (C-section) was first used in the 1600s as an alternative to vaginal delivery in cases of emergency childbirth. Over the centuries, significant breakthroughs have been made to the point where C-section delivery is now safe. It is also the only way women at risk for complications later in their pregnancies can deliver their children.

When is a C-Section Performed?

There are three circumstances when a C-section might happen:

1. Emergency

If your or your baby's health is in jeopardy and the baby needs to be born right away, an emergency operation may be necessary. For instance, if the infant is born feet first, has a cord wrapped around their neck, or isn't receiving enough oxygen, then a C-section will be essential.

2. Elective C-Section

Suppose there are increased risks with vaginal birth (your baby is giant, or you have pregnancy-caused diabetes), and your doctor believes it would be safer for your baby to be delivered via C-section. In that case, you may be advised to have an elective C-section.

3. Maternal Request C-Section

As mentioned, some C-sections are considered elective, meaning they are requested before labor. However, there can also be a maternal request for a C-section, which is when you seek a C-section for yourself. Although there is no legal entitlement to a C-section in the United States, it is a mother's choice how she gives birth.

Cesarean Procedure

Time is of the essence in an emergency C-section. The aim is to get the baby out as quickly as possible, as your life or the life of your infant may be in jeopardy. The time it takes from the start of surgery until delivery can be as little as one minute.

Suppose you received an epidural during your vaginal birth attempt. In that case, your anesthesiologist might be able to give you enough drugs through your epidural to keep you awake during the C-section. If you did not have an epidural, your doctor might have to administer general anesthesia to you (which means you won't be conscious), so you will meet your child as soon as you wake up.

Non-emergency C-sections usually start within 30 to 60 minutes of your doctor's decision. You will most likely be awake for this C-section and will greet your baby right away. You'll be given a spinal anesthetic, an epidural, or combined spinal-epidural anesthesia (CSE) to ensure you don't feel any discomfort.

Pros of Cesarean Birth

A woman may opt for a C-section if she is afraid of giving birth vaginally, impacting her delivery experience.

When compared to women who deliver vaginally, women who have C-sections are less likely to experience urine incontinence and pelvic organ prolapse.

A surgical birth can be planned on time, making it more convenient and predictable than a vaginal birth and labor.

A C-section can be lifesaving if the baby or mother is in danger.

Cons of Cesarean Birth

After a C-section, the mother, on average, needs to stay for two to four days in the hospital, compared to one to two days for vaginal deliveries.

Because the skin and nerves surrounding the surgical scar need time to heal, the recovery period is also longer, and there may be agonizing pain and discomfort in the abdomen.

A C-section raises the chance of post-delivery complications, such as incision site pain or infection, as well as longer-lasting soreness.

There is a higher risk of blood loss during a C-section.

Women are three times more likely to die during a cesarean birth than a vaginal birth, owing to blood clots, infections, and anesthesia-related problems.

C-section babies are more likely to develop breathing issues at birth and even later in life.

There may also be a higher chance of subsequent pregnancy difficulties, such as uterine rupture or placental abnormalities.

Medical Reasons for a Cesarean

Your doctor may schedule a cesarean birth in advance of your due date. It may also be required in an emergency during or before labor.

Some of the most prevalent medical causes for a cesarean section are listed below.

Abnormal Position of Baby: Babies should be placed headfirst near the birth canal to have a healthy vaginal birth. However, newborns have a habit of flipping the script.

A breech birth happens when the baby's feet or buttocks face the canal, whereas a transverse birth happens when the baby's shoulder or side faces the canal. Cesarean delivery may be the safest option in certain instances, especially for mothers carrying multiple children.

Prolonged Labor: According to the Centers for Disease Control and Prevention (CDC), roughly one-third of cesareans are caused by prolonged labor, often known as "failure to progress" or "stalled labor." They are prescribed when a new mother has been in labor for more than 20 hours and an experienced mother for 14 hours or more.

Premature labor can be caused by various factors, including babies who are too big for the delivery canal and sluggish cervical thinning. In certain situations, doctors may recommend a cesarean section to avert complications.

Birth Defects: Doctors often opt to deliver children with specific birth problems, such as excess fluid in the brain or genetic heart diseases, via cesarean section to avoid delivery risks.

Chronic Health Condition: If a woman has a chronic health problem, such as high blood pressure, heart disease, or gestational diabetes, she may need a cesarean delivery. When one of these diseases exists, vaginal delivery may be risky for the mother.

Carrying Twins or Triplets: Carrying multiples during pregnancy can have various dangers. It might lead to long labor, which can be stressful for the mother. It is also possible that one or more babies are in the wrong position. In either case, a cesarean section is frequently the safest delivery option.

Cord Prolapse: A cord prolapse happens when the umbilical cord falls through the cervix just before the infant is delivered. As a result, the blood supply to the infant may be reduced, putting the baby's health in danger.

Cord prolapse is a dangerous disorder that necessitates an emergency cesarean birth despite its rarity.

Cephalopelvic Disproportion (CPD):

Cephalopelvic disproportion occurs when the baby's head or body is too big to travel through the birth canal or when the mother's pelvis is too narrow to deliver the baby naturally. In either situation, the baby will not be able to pass through the vaginal opening safely, so a C-section is recommended.

C-Section: What to Expect from Recovery

A C-section is a major surgical procedure, so it necessitates the use of an anesthetic. Unless you require an emergency C-section, the type of anesthesia you will receive will allow you to be awake during the procedure. You may have to spend the rest of the day in bed.

It would help if you planned on spending 2 to 4 days in the hospital after having a C-section. A total recuperation time of up to 6 weeks is also possible.

You may not have any soreness right after the procedure. However, once the anesthetic wears off, you may experience pain, particularly around the incision. Expect to be exhausted. You may also require assistance in lifting your newborn.

Women have also reported experiencing constipation, cramping, bloating, and nausea after going through a C-section.

Some Myths About Cesarean Birth

Myth 1: You can't have skin-to-skin time after a C-section

For many new mothers, skin-to-skin contact is essential. It entails placing your newborn infant on your chest right after birth, and it provides you and your child with a bonding opportunity as well as other health benefits.

Skin-to-skin contact facilitates initiation to breastfeeding within the first hour after delivery, too. This is critical for a good start of life for the newborn as they can get the most nutritious first milk, 'colostrum,' which is good for their health. Doctors, nurses, and midwives should encourage skin-to-skin time after a C-section and have the mother initiate breastfeeding as soon as she is conscious.

Many women worry that because they are connected to machines, wearing a hospital gown, or under anesthesia, they won't be able to enjoy skin-to-skin time after their C-section. This is *not* true.

Myth 2: You can't deliver vaginally after a C-section

Your doctor will make an incision in your abdomen and uterus during a C-section. After your baby is born, the incision will be sutured.

A frequent fallacy surrounding C-sections is that having the operation means you will never be able to give birth vaginally again if you get pregnant later. This is not true.

If you are not expected to have any complications or if your baby is not at risk in your subsequent pregnancy, then you can quickly go for a vaginal delivery.

Myth 3: C-sections make birth easier

A popular myth is that opting for a C-section can save you the agony experienced during vaginal delivery and lower your risk of complications like vaginal prolapse.

A C-section is not uncomfortable when it is taking place; however, once the anesthesia or epidural wears off, the pain can take some time to fade away, perhaps as long as a few weeks.

Myth 4: C-sections will reduce the risk of prolapse

The condition vaginal prolapse occurs when the vaginal walls become flexible. Because the vaginal wall can no longer support them, the uterus, rectum, bladder, urethra, and small bowel begin to fall out of their natural locations. This condition, however, is a concern whether the baby is born vaginally or via cesarean section.

Myth 5: It is okay to have a lot of C-sections

If a woman has undergone repeated C-sections, there is cause for concern. After three to four caesareans, the chance of complications rises. Repeat caesareans can raise the risk of placenta accreta, a dangerous pregnancy disorder in which the placenta's blood arteries and other elements grow through the previous C-section scarring and adjacent structures.

Myth 6: Mothers who deliver via C-section will maintain their body figure more quickly compared to those who deliver vaginally.

This misconception is based on the belief that C-sections prevent the physical changes associated with vaginal birth, such as stretching or tearing of the pelvic muscles and tissues.

However, medical evidence does not support this myth. Regardless of the mode of delivery, pregnancy brings about significant changes in a woman's body. These changes include weight gain, hormonal fluctuations, and body shape and size alterations. The recovery process and return to pre-pregnancy body shape depend on various factors, such as genetics, diet, exercise, and overall health, rather than the type of delivery.

Myth 7: You Can't Breastfeed After a C-Section

While some mothers might face initial challenges breastfeeding after a C-section, many successfully breastfeed with proper support and guidance.

Myth 8: C-Sections Don't Allow for Immediate Bonding

Some believe that mothers who have C-sections can't bond with their babies immediately. However, many hospitals now practice skin-to-skin contact and breastfeeding shortly after C-sections, fostering early bonding.

Your Right to Choose

Both vaginal and C-section births have risks and potential problems. Mothers have complete autonomy over how they want their babies to be delivered. Mothers who choose to have a cesarean birth are more likely to undergo a C-section for subsequent pregnancies as well.

CHAPTER 5

⋘⋘⋘⋘⋘

THE BIRTH

Jair's birth was a medically quick emergency process. Inspite of the experience of tremendous anxiety, helplessness, loss of control, and agony during pregnancy, childbirth became a traumatic event. In a preterm birth circumstance like mine, many of these fears can be present.

Truthfully, my biggest fear was having a c-section for the birth of Jair. I prayed against it most of the time because there were risk factors associated with short stature, poor appetite and anxiety during the first pregnancy, and a busy schedule for the mother. Nonetheless, the inevitable happened.

As a result, giving birth prematurely and then spending time in the ICU was highly stressful for me, especially with the knowledge that my baby was in the nursery without me. According to studies, women who deliver preterm have much greater levels of stress and depression than those who deliver on time.[11]

It makes no difference whether a mother goes into early labor spontaneously or has her preterm baby delivered by surgery; the effect is the same. What counts is the mother's and baby's health. This is something we will talk about in this chapter.

Allaying Fears of Giving Birth to a Preterm Baby

Tokophobia is the fear of pregnancy. It is explained as a severe case of anxiety that may cause many women to become scared of childbirth and, as a result, to avoid pregnancy despite having a strong desire for a child.

It is probably reasonable to be concerned or anxious about labor. Women with tokophobia, who want a baby but cannot overcome their fear, may even terminate their pregnancy. This is why a mother with a preterm baby should fully know about her child's birth and safety measures.

The intensity of the child's medical risk factors and parental mental health is recognized to significantly impact the emotional, social, cognitive, and physical development of children. Several studies have investigated maternal depression after preterm birth.

---

[11] Debra S Lefkowitz, Chiara Baxt, Jacquelyn R Evans. Prevalence and correlates of posttraumatic stress and postpartum depression in parents of infants in the Neonatal Intensive Care Unit (NICU). *J Clin Psychol Med Settings.* 2010 Sep;17(3):230-7. doi: 10.1007/s10880-010-9202-7.

According to studies, preterm mothers have a higher risk of depression than term mothers in the first year after giving birth, and mothers with extremely low-birth-weight babies have a higher risk of depression in the first year after giving birth.[12]

Furthermore, persistent parental depressive symptoms are a substantial predictor of child failure in several investigations of children born prematurely.

Even if the pregnancy has gone well and the mother is in good health, all mothers and fathers worry about the birth in the back of their minds. Therefore, you should be aware of the following things:

Your Birth Plan May Be Altered If You Have a Preterm Baby

Because many mothers don't begin antenatal classes until around the thirtieth week, they might not have developed a birth plan or even thought about how they want to deliver the baby.

If you have a birth plan in place, having your baby earlier than you thought may require you to alter some of your plans. For instance, you will need to go to the hospital instead of delivering the baby to a midwife-led unit or home. Suppose your preferred hospital does not offer specialist facilities for preterm newborns. In that case, you may need to be moved to

12 Semra Worrall, Sergio A. Silverio, Victoria M. Fallon. The relationship between prematurity and maternal mental health during the first postpartum year. *Journal of Neonatal Nursing.* Volume 29, Issue 3, June 2023, Pages 511-518.

one that does if issues arise, such as if your obstetrician or midwife is worried about you or your baby's health, you may require birth assistance, like an immediate cesarean.

Medications

If you are in labor, you can be offered tocolysis, an obstetrical procedure that helps slow labor. The medication provided is only suitable if you deliver one baby and not twins, etc. You also must be aware that doctors may also use steroid injections to aid in developing your baby's lungs and that magnesium sulfate may be used to encourage brain development.

Having a C-Section If You Go into Premature Labor

You may be confused if you want to have a cesarean or a natural delivery despite your doctor suggesting the best choice. Doctors may likely advocate a vaginal birth rather than a cesarean section for early births. This could be because the womb is too small for a typical horizontal cut, necessitating a vertical cut by your doctor. This raises the likelihood that future pregnancies will also require cesarean sections as well.

Even if you intended on having a vaginal delivery, you might be advised to have a cesarean section if:

- ❖ Your healthcare team is concerned about your and your baby's health, so the baby must be delivered immediately.

❖ Your baby is not in a head-down position.

❖ The labor is not progressing

Before you give your consent, talk to your doctor about the pros and cons of having a C-section.

Having a Vaginal Birth in Preterm Labor

The fundamental distinction between full-term and preterm labor is that the latter may be quicker. During preterm labor, healthcare professionals will also closely monitor you and the baby and constantly check the baby's position. Early in pregnancy, breech newborns are more common. By 36–37 weeks, most newborns have naturally moved into the headfirst position.

In addition, your medical staff will be prepared to execute emergency procedures.

The Stages of Labor

The latent phase occurs before labor begins, usually when your cervix softens and thins as it prepares to open (dilate). Your contractions may be few, mild, or irregular during this period.

Labor is typically divided into three stages:

Stage 1 — Also known as established labor, this is the first stage of labor. You reach this stage when your cervix expands to at least 5cm, and your contractions become more robust and regular.

Stage 2 — Once your cervix is fully dilated and your womb muscles tighten and relax to push the baby out, you are in the second stage.

Stage 3 — When you have had your baby but still need to deliver the placenta, you are in the third stage of labor. During your pregnancy, your midwife will discuss the many choices for delivering the placenta and the benefits and drawbacks of each.

Assisted Birth

If there are any worries about your or your baby's health, or if the baby is not coming out as planned, you may require assistance in delivering your baby.

If this occurs, your medical team may advise you to have an assisted birth. During the last stage of labor, the doctor will use special instruments (forceps or ventouse) to assist in the baby's delivery.

Smooth metal devices that resemble giant spoons or tongs are known as forceps. They are curved to fit around the head of your child. The doctor will place them around your baby's head with care, wait until you have a contraction, and then ask you to push while they gently pull to assist in the delivery of your baby.

A ventouse (vacuum extractor) attaches a hard or soft plastic or metal cup to your baby's head via suction. When you're having a contraction, the doctor will encourage you to push while they gently pull to help you deliver your baby.

Both the ventouse and the forceps are effective and safe. If you are less than 36 weeks pregnant, ventilation is not recommended since the baby's skull is softer, increasing the risk of injury. If your doctor or midwife needs to use forceps or a ventouse to help deliver your baby, they will always ask for your permission first.

Pain Relief

You may require pain management if you have a vaginal birth. If you need further pain relief, your midwife should provide you with gas and air (Entonox) or an epidural.

If you are already in advanced labor, you may be warned against taking pethidine, diamorphine, or other opiates. This is because if your baby is born soon after the medications are administered, they may harm the baby's breathing, which may be amplified if they are preterm.

Delayed Cord Clamping

If possible, the medical staff will wait at least one minute following the birth before clamping the chord. Blood, oxygen, and nutrients (especially iron necessary to prevent anemia) will continue to flow through the cord to your baby at this period. It's not always possible to postpone cord clamping, especially in cases where your newborn requires breathing assistance.

After Your Baby Is Born

When your baby arrives, the healthcare staff will immediately examine their condition and treat them if needed. The level of care will be determined by the time the baby is gestated.

If your newborn needs immediate attention, you may be unable to hold them immediately after birth. This might be a trying moment, but you will be given valuable time to bond with your baby as soon as it is safe and possible.

Except for the low birth weight and small size, Jair was healthy and physically strong. Hence, the midwife handed him to me immediately after delivery, and I had the first opportunity to hold him and dedicate him to God. After cleaning, the midwife handed him over to the neonatal nurse, who took him to the nursery for further care.

Your Mental Health

Every mother wishes for a healthy, uneventful pregnancy, labor, and delivery. When this does not occur, it cannot be very pleasant. Please don't fear expressing your feelings to your healthcare provider; they will not judge you. It is usual for your mental health to suffer after delivering a child, and your healthcare providers are aware of this.

It is better to focus on the baby and your health and refrain from meeting people. Sometimes, this can be exhausting, as one of our interviewees mentioned that people may ask questions like, "How are you managing?"

As I mentioned from experience, "People who came later to see Jair would say, "You have a small baby" and I would feel bad, people not knowing that the baby wasn't full term. And being preterm, he was too dark because he is preterm. This is why we suggest not engaging with people, especially during these challenging times when your mental health is already too low.

Facing the ICU

A neonatal intensive care unit (NICU) can be a frightening and challenging setting for your child, you, and your family. Make the NICU/ICU your zone by spending time with your baby. It can be an emotional and stressful experience to be a parent of a newborn in the neonatal intensive care unit (NICU)/intensive care nursery (ICN). We understand how essential it is to you that your baby's therapies are as comfortable as possible.

The professional team caring for your infant constantly works to make therapy less painful for all babies. The objective is for you to be entirely satisfied with how your baby's discomfort was managed while they were in the NICU.

For the first days when the mother was still in the ICU, I spent most of my time between the NICU and the ICU expressing breast milk and giving it to the neonatal nurse to feed Jair. I also went there to the

NICU to check and speak with him. When the mother was discharged from the ICU and regained some strength, she visited Jair in the NICU, where she could sit and breastfeed him until he was discharged to join us in the general ward. This was necessary for bonding and ensuring the baby got sufficient breast milk.

Make the NICU Space Your Own

To distinguish your baby's space from other babies, you can bring items from home, use gifts from others, or hang photos of yourself and your baby's siblings. However, remember that too much clutter can make it harder to care for your newborn.

Hospital employees and volunteers frequently put on special events. For example, Santa visits during Christmas, and the crew decorates. By putting up decorations yourself, you can commemorate a significant occasion, such as a family birthday, religious event, or your baby's expected birth date.

The hospital put a name tag on Jair's leg, and luckily, there were only three babies at the time he was admitted to the NICU. This eased our ability to identify and interact with him. The nurses were so kind and caring that they could not deny us the opportunity to see the baby whenever we wanted.

Spending Time with Your Baby

It is easy to feel overwhelmed in the NICU. If you have any questions, it is okay to ask hospital professionals to clarify things for you in terms you can understand. You can jot down key details to help yourself remember them.

Developing a rapport with medical personnel might make it easier to ask questions and keep yourself informed. You could meet with two or three medical professionals regularly to discuss your baby's progress. You can do this during ward rounds. Plan to be in the NICU while the staff does your baby's "care," if possible. You can start by learning and then gradually take over the care of your infant.

Jair's neonatal nurse oriented us on how to care for him, including conducting KMC, interacting with him, and changing his diapers and clothes. This was helpful, given his special needs. She initially supervised our care for the baby to ensure we were doing the right thing.

You become a part of their life by doing little things for your baby. You will also learn how to handle your child as they prefer, and they will learn to recognize you. This is an excellent method to establish confidence in your ability to care for them.

Friends and extended relatives can visit some NICUs, but not all can. If your friends and relatives visit, you can begin introducing your child to their new family and friends. Visitors can join you for a meal or sit with your infant while you eat or walk. Most importantly, they support you as you support your child.

For us, only the dad and mom could access Jair while he was in the NICU. This was done to safeguard him and other babies against infections from many people visiting. The hospital's standard permits only parents or known primary caregivers to access babies admitted to the NICU.

Taking the Time to Relax

Long shifts in the NICU can be tedious and exhausting. Take turns in everything you do caring for your child, leaving the hospital for a break. You can get your body moving while also getting sun on your face when you're outside in the fresh air. The noise in the NICU might be bothersome, especially if you're nervous or suffering from a headache. So, going out for short periods can help alleviate any tension.

Try mindfulness, breathing exercises, or muscle relaxation if your days in the hospital are exhausting and stressful. These activities can be done while sitting next to your infant. If you find these exercises challenging to execute independently, you can download a smartphone application to guide you through them.

We did everything regarding Jair's care in the hospital. I spent most of the time providing KMC to Jair when the mother rested. She did the same to give me some time to rest. We agreed to have ourselves only access him to safeguard him against any possible infection from other visitors.

Caring for a Preterm Baby

Right from birth until six months, Jair was fed only breast milk and was prescribed medicines, including supplements. This was important for catch-up growth and strengthening of some weak organs like the lungs and the heart. Despite the nurse at the NICU asking me to get infant formula for him, I refused to do so. Instead, I hand-expressed breastmilk from the mom and fed him until she was stable to breastmilk. We knew the value of breast milk to Jair in his unique condition and could not let anyone give him formula, drinks, or food.

When our baby started complementary feeding at six months, he was a jolly man full of energy. He brings energy to our home. And He is a very handsome man, I can say. So, all kinds of support we received from health care professionals, family, and spiritual colleagues have been helpful. And I think personally, I most of the time forget that He was a low-birth-weight baby when I look at him right now. But if one had not seen him before, you cannot see He is a preemie baby.

As critical as this care is for our baby's survival, moving them to a special-care nursery was a difficult transition for us. Stella especially missed the earlier experience of holding, breastfeeding, and connecting with him shortly after delivery, on top of all the stress about her and his health. She couldn't hold or touch him at any time, and she couldn't keep him in the same room with him.

To cope with the stress of the situation, I was very present. As mentioned above, I always saw our baby as quickly as possible after delivery and participated as much as possible in their care.

I spent as much time with Jair as the medical personnel allowed me to, and it was the most precious moment of our lives. So, from that experience, I must say, touch them regularly, even if you can't hold them yet (until he's/she's stable). When the newborns' organ systems do not require considerable support, many critical care units allow parents to undertake skin-to-skin care for their babies or call it kangarooing, which we did at every opportunity and yielded terrific results, especially for Stella, who joined us two weeks later.

You may also feed them as soon as your doctor permits you. The nutritionists and nurses will teach you how to breastfeed or bottle-feed your baby, depending on the infant's needs and preferences.

For some preterm babies, fluids may be administered intravenously or through a feeding tube that enters the stomach through the mouth or nose. On the other hand, your breast milk offers the best possible nutrition, as it contains antibodies and other compounds that boost your child's immune system and help them fight infection.

If your preterm infant cannot nurse at the breast, you can pump breast milk and feed it through a tube or bottle. Your baby should be seen as any other child. Nonetheless, to maintain a good supply of milk, mothers of preterm newborns may need to keep using a breast pump while nursing.

It may be difficult for you to come back home before your infant; however, keep in mind that your baby is in good hands and that you are welcome to visit them as often as you want. You can utilize your time away from the hospital to recover, prepare your house and family for your baby's arrival, and read a book for parents about caring for preterm babies.

Even after you have returned home, the more involved you are in your infant's recuperation and the more contact you have with them during this period, the better you will feel about the situation and the simpler it will be to care for them once they leave the special care nursery.

Touch, hold, and cradle your infant as soon as your doctor says it is fine; your pediatrician may be involved in, or at least aware of, your infant's initial care. As a result, he will be able to answer most of your inquiries.

When your baby can breathe independently, maintain their body temperature, be fed by bottle or breast, and gain weight gradually, they will be ready to go home.

The main reason we decided to share our story was to deliver an important message to build the capacities of parents to deal with situations like preterm or low birth rates to ensure that the baby is supported to grow well and become as normal as any other baby who might have been born during the due time. Parents should also build social support for themselves and interact with other parents who have gone through preterm delivery.

Lastly, I can say that the nutritional care, medical care, and social support we received were instrumental in helping us through this journey and getting him where he is right now. Jair rapidly gained weight up to 6 kg in the first four months.

Our Experience Feeding Jair

Jair was put on supplementary multivitamins and minerals, including vitamin A and iron, from day one because of his preterm birth and low birth weight. This ensured he got good nutrition to promote quick growth and development. In addition to these prescribed supplements, we exclusively breastfed him for six months without giving him any other fluids or food. He had no issues with breastfeeding, as he had a good appetite.

At six months, we introduced complementary foods to him, starting with nutrient-dense fluids and porridges consistent with his taste. In preparation for this, I had to get an easy-to-use book for the mother to follow in preparing the right quality of complementary food so that all the required nutrients were included. Jair loved his food and ate with joy. In the early days of complementary feeding, he specifically liked juice, watermelon, mangoes, pineapples, water, and porridge.

As he grew older and learned to chew more, he loved beef/goat meat/chicken like his mother. He enjoyed all sorts of food, but we struggled to feed him vegetables. We had to devise ways to make him eat them through, for instance, blending them into source and juices. As we gave him complementary food, we continued with multivitamins and minerals, although he did not like medication. So, it was a struggle to get him to take these. We dewormed him for one year and continued with the battle of giving him the supplements we needed. He needed them to keep healthy.

Advice to Mothers That May Give or Have Given Birth to a Preterm Baby

I gave birth to a preterm baby and, according to experience, laid down some advice that can help a mother out both emotionally and physically. Both parents should remain positive no matter what because that helped us immensely during this experience. Parents should be okay with these things that are happening. They are going to happen anyway. They always happen. If you find yourself in any challenging situation in life, just be optimistic about it and run the race.

Secondly, don't blame yourself. Don't ask yourself questions such as what went wrong. Mothers should know these things are natural and unavoidable, but more so, expecting mothers to keep visiting hospitals. I used to ask, "Do village mothers also have such a problem?" because I wondered if a mother in a village had such a problem, how would they go about it, and how would they take care of such a preterm child?

Therefore, my advice is to use the little that you have and visit the nearby hospitals often. Attending your Antenatal appointments. It is essential: imagine what would happen if I wasn't doing any antenatal.

I also encourage women to get specialized doctors who know their medical history and pregnancy history. I think if I didn't have an obstetrician who knew my medical history well, I would have been messed up somehow. I'm against the concept of finding a new obstetrician for the baby's care and delivery during each pregnancy.

Our Experience with Other Mothers in the Hospital

The experience I had even when we were still in the hospital was of one young lady who had overstayed in the hospital with a preterm and did not have anyone to guide her. She had trouble with breastfeeding and acceptance of her baby.

Jair's mother and she met accidentally in the hospital and shared their stories. They exchanged contacts and continued to encourage each other. Therefore, mothers of such children must look for those who have walked in their shoes to support them. This is more critical for first-time mothers.

It is critical for the spouses to also be there for them; they are looking for acceptance and not judgment, and their spouses are the starting point. I can imagine what could have happened to her if I had acted otherwise from the time of birth, including her being in the ICU, KMC, etc. Spouses/husbands should continue to play the protective, educative, and provider roles to these mothers, especially if they are first-time mothers.

However, it is crucial to get timely, appropriate counseling in case either or both parents fail to accept their situation. Addressing this early will save the baby's life and create a feel-good environment.

CHAPTER 6

✦✦✦✦✦

INTRODUCING YOURSELF TO YOUR NEWBORN

Forming an attachment with an infant in the ICU may not always feel natural, but it is feasible. Once the baby is finally home, it's time to comprehend the unique identity of this little individual. The task of welcoming a preterm baby home and taking responsibility for their needs is a demanding endeavor for the parents. Parents must start planning for the long-term care of their preterm child right from the hospital's ICU.

This demands psychological, emotional, physical, and spiritual adaptations, without which the burden on the parents and caregivers might become overwhelming. Assistance from the medical and counseling teams is instrumental in achieving this while the parents are still in the hospital, anticipating their discharge and return home.

Welcoming Your Preterm Baby Home

The experience of bringing a newborn home for the first time can seem formidable, but for parents of preterm babies, the challenge can be incredibly intense. To facilitate the transition from hospital to home, consider these guidelines:

Coming to terms with the situation:

The initial step involves reconciling with the reality of having a preterm baby. The unexpected nature of a preterm birth can be challenging to digest for many parents. This denial can adversely impact the baby's care. Parents must accept preterm birth to provide the best possible care for their baby. The preterm birth experience can be challenging and emotionally strenuous for parents, bringing forth feelings of guilt, fear, and anxiety. However, recognizing the reality of a preterm birth can assist parents in becoming more active in their child's care, better prepared for possible complications, and more effective advocates for their baby's needs.

For us, accepting that he was born preterm was not an easy feat, but the understanding that the outcome could have been worse helped us embrace the situation more readily. We considered the grim statistics surrounding complicated pregnancies in Africa and felt fortunate. High rates of maternal and neonatal mortality mark Africa, with many of these deaths arising from complications during pregnancy, childbirth, or the postpartum period.

According to the WHO, in 2019, sub-Saharan Africa reported a maternal mortality ratio of 542 deaths per 100,000 live births. This ratio is more than 50 times higher than that in high-income countries. Similarly, the neonatal mortality rate in sub-Saharan Africa was 27 deaths per 1,000 live births, almost quadruple the rate in high-income countries.

Witnessing his strength and maturity despite his preterm birth was inspiring enough for us to come to terms with the situation. Subsequently, I found it easier to mentally, physically, and spiritually prepare for a new life of caring for him and his mother. I realized that they both needed my support now more than ever.

It took the mother longer to accept the preterm birth, but I was able to encourage her. We were ready to welcome and care for our baby when we left the hospital. The mother served as an inspiration to a few other mothers facing similar or worse predicaments due to preterm birth.

Educate Yourself

Familiarizing yourself with your preterm baby's specific needs and medical conditions is crucial in providing the best care. This includes understanding potential health risks associated with preterm birth, such as respiratory distress syndrome, jaundice, and infections, and knowing about the treatments and interventions necessary to address these issues. The more informed you are, the more confidence you will have in caring for your baby.

Engage with your baby's healthcare team to understand their recommendations and any necessary medications, treatments, or therapies. It is equally important to steer clear of unfounded information, which can jeopardize the health of your preterm baby. Always seek accurate and trustworthy information from reliable sources, such as your baby's healthcare providers and reputable medical websites.

Besides interacting with healthcare professionals, parents can also find solace in joining support groups or reputable online communities. These groups allow parents to connect with other parents of preterm babies and exchange experiences and information. These groups can provide much-needed emotional support and practical advice on caring for a preterm baby.

As first-time parents of a preterm baby, we discovered that understanding his specific needs and medical conditions was fundamental to his optimal care. Fortunately, our healthcare team of highly experienced neonatologists, pediatricians, medical officers, nurses, midwives, and counselors all helped us learn the best ways to care for our baby.

As a nutritionist, I was already aware of the nutritional requirements of a preterm baby. However, it was particularly helpful to understand the importance of breast milk and its role in reducing infection risks, promoting growth, and providing essential nutrients.

There were instances when we had to politely decline advice from the medical team that contradicted the Ministry of Health recommendations. One of the ICU nurses suggested that we purchase infant formula for the baby, but I knew that breast milk was the best option for him. I ensured he was initiated to breastfeed within the first hour of birth by expressing breast milk from his mother, who was still in the ICU. We also exclusively breastfed him for six months, as required by the Ministry of Health, despite his being a preterm birth.

We also invested in the literature on nutrition and health care for babies, including preterm, to bolster our knowledge on caring for such delicate infants. However, we were mindful to verify any information we came across to avoid hearsay and unproven remedies that could potentially harm our baby. We regularly communicated with our baby's doctors, nurses, and therapists to ensure we understood their recommendations and any necessary medications, treatments, or therapies.

Create a safe environment

In retrospect, our journey underscored the value of self-education regarding the unique requirements and health conditions of our preterm baby, which empowered us to give him the best possible care. We also found support groups and reputable online communities invaluable. These platforms facilitate connections with other parents of preterm babies, providing an avenue to exchange experiences and information.

The emotional backing and practical advice we received from these communities were essential for our baby's care. Creating a safe environment involved ensuring that our home was well-prepared with everything needed for our baby's well-being, such as an appropriate crib, a clean and tranquil space, and proper baby-proofing measures. Consultation with healthcare professionals was necessary to identify specific safety requirements for our baby, like monitoring devices or oxygen equipment.

Before the preterm birth of our son, Jair, we had undertaken basic preparations. However, the advent of our preterm baby required us to modify certain aspects. For example, he couldn't be in his crib in the early days at home due to his need for extra warmth and care. This necessitated the mother's adjustment to sharing our bed with him for several months. We procured extra warm bedding for him, thermometers, syringes, multivitamins, and other essential items. We ensured easy access to these supplies, allowing us to handle emergencies swiftly.

Beyond medical supplies, we also prioritized our preterm baby's nutritional needs. We ensured a substantial stock of breast milk in our freezer and had the necessary equipment for expressing milk and feeding our baby. We also sought advice from healthcare professionals to provide our preterm baby with the correct amount and type of nutrients.

Moreover, we educated ourselves on Kangaroo Mother Care (KMC), a technique of holding a preterm baby skin-to-skin against the mother's bare chest. This method has demonstrated numerous benefits for preterm infants, including better temperature regulation, improved oxygen saturation, stress and pain reduction, and enhanced breastfeeding success.

Initially skeptical about KMC, we soon discovered its merits. We placed our preterm baby on the bare chest of the mother and father, with his head turned to one side to facilitate easy breathing. We then securely wrapped him in a blanket or clothing to maintain his warmth.

Our healthcare providers recommended KMC thrice daily for at least an hour, but we often extended these sessions, especially initially. It was a profound bonding experience for us, and we also observed its positive impact on our baby's well-being. KMC calmed and contented him, improved his sleep, and facilitated feeding.

In addition to KMC, we also took other steps to ensure our preterm baby's safety and well-being at home. We kept our home free from hazards like sharp objects or loose cords, constantly monitored his temperature, and watched for signs of distress such as difficulty breathing or low oxygen saturation.

Preparing your home for a preterm baby involves securing all necessary equipment, supplies, and a suitable sleeping arrangement. Consulting with healthcare professionals can assist in identifying your baby's specific safety requirements. Training in Kangaroo Mother Care is crucial, as is having all the necessary multivitamins and other essentials for your baby's care.

Preparing for visitors is crucial

Limit the number of visitors during the initial weeks and insist that everyone interacting with your baby adheres to proper hygiene practices. This includes washing hands, abstaining from visits when unwell, and avoiding smoking around the baby, thereby safeguarding your baby's delicate immune system.

Upon our arrival home, we were inundated with calls from friends and family, all excited to welcome the new family member. Despite the challenge of turning away visitors, especially close family and friends, we knew we had to adhere to the medical advice we received. It was crucial to communicate to them that our baby's fragile health necessitated limited exposure to the outside world and time to build his immune system.

Sticking to our plan was challenging, given the cultural norms around newborn visitations. However, by being assertive yet respectful, we explained that our baby wasn't ready for interaction. We kept everyone updated on our baby's progress, sharing photos and videos to ensure they remained involved in his life.

Although limiting visitors was challenging, we knew it was for our baby's best interest and our mental health. Following the healthcare team's advice and maintaining a clean, risk-free home environment, we saw our baby grow stronger daily. When the time was right, we welcomed visitors, confident we'd done our utmost to protect our baby.

Regrettably, criticism and judgment are everyday experiences for parents of preterm babies, often coming from family, friends, and even strangers. This judgment can be incredibly stressful for parents already navigating the emotional and physical challenges of having a preterm baby. It's, therefore, vital to set boundaries with visitors and communicate your needs and expectations.

Parents should not feel pressured to allow visitors to interact with their preterm baby if it feels risky or uncomfortable. Neither should they feel compelled to justify their decisions. Prioritizing your baby's and your well-being over others' expectations is entirely acceptable.

Support from those who have been through similar experiences, such as support groups or online communities, can be highly beneficial. These resources provide understanding and validation, helping to alleviate some of the stress and judgment from others.

Build a support network

Engage with friends, family, and healthcare professionals who can provide guidance, aid, and encouragement when required. Participate in local or online support groups for parents of preterm babies to connect with those facing similar hurdles and exchange experiences.

Navigating parenthood with a preterm baby, as we can attest, necessitates a solid support system. Upon bringing Jair home from the hospital, we were novices in handling the demands of a preterm baby. As none of our family members had a history of preterm births, we initially felt isolated. However, we quickly realized the indispensability of a support system.

We contacted our friends, family, and healthcare professionals, who became our support pillars, offering crucial advice, aid, and moral encouragement when we needed it the most. We sought emotional comfort from our family and help with household chores. Our friends became our sounding board, always ready to lend an ear, assist with practical needs like meals, or run errands for us.

The healthcare professionals at the hospital where Jair was born became our constant resource. Their availability for consultation and assistance imbued us with the confidence to look after Jair at home. We diligently adhered to their instructions and never hesitated to seek their help with any questions or concerns.

Joining a local support group for parents of preterm babies also proved immensely beneficial. The group allowed us to connect with other parents navigating similar experiences. The opportunity to share our journey and learn from those who had walked in our shoes was invaluable. The group provided a sense of validation and understanding that we couldn't always find among our friends and family who hadn't experienced parenting a preterm baby.

In summary, a robust support system is paramount when caring for a preterm baby. Though it can feel isolating and challenging, the presence of a caring network that offers practical and emotional support can make a world of difference.

Adapting Your Life to Your Preterm Baby's Needs

Caring for a preterm baby can be a daunting and emotional journey. Their small size and potential health complications can make parenting seem overwhelming. Additionally, setting routines for a preterm baby is often more difficult due to their frequent feeding needs and possible health issues such as jaundice or colic. Here are a few tips to foster a harmonious home environment:

Embrace patience and flexibility

Recognize that your baby's routine may not always correspond with your own, and be prepared to adjust your schedule accordingly. It's crucial to remember that preterm babies might take longer to establish regular sleep and feeding routines; hence, patience is essential.

As first-time parents of a preterm baby, we quickly discovered that our little one had a unique schedule that often didn't align with ours. This required us to practice patience and flexibility with our daily routines, putting aside our expectations and adjusting our schedules when necessary.

Though challenging, we realized that our baby's well-being was paramount, which meant placing our own needs and preferences on hold to ensure our child received the necessary care. This included waking at odd hours for feeding or comfort or alternating responsibilities to ensure we both got adequate rest. For example, we provided our baby Kangaroo Mother Care (KMC) in shifts, as it was pretty taxing to do alone. Our sleeping positions also changed to accommodate our little ones.

This experience deepened our bond as we collaborated to care for our child, enhancing our communication and mutual support through challenging times. Our love for our baby brought us closer as parents, especially during periods of intense colic, when our combined effort was essential for soothing him. Over time, as we remained patient and flexible, our baby began to develop his patterns and routines.

Prioritize sleep

Ensure that both you and your baby get adequate sleep. Establish a serene and comfortable sleeping environment and consider a bedtime routine to signal your baby that it's time to sleep. Share responsibilities with your spouse to ensure that you both get sufficient rest, and try napping when your baby does to optimize your sleep opportunities.

Achieving sufficient sleep was one of our most significant challenges. Establishing a regular sleep routine seemed impossible, with our baby requiring frequent feeding and care. However, we learned that sleep was crucial for our and our babies' well-being.

We tried to create a calm sleeping environment for our child, setting up a safe, comfortable, and soothing sleeping area. We established a bedtime routine with soft music and dim lights to signal sleep time.

We alternated sleep schedules to ensure we both had enough rest, sometimes enlisting the help of family or friends for a few hours to get some much-needed rest. We also adopted the habit of napping when the baby did, even briefly, to maximize our rest. As the baby grew and adapted to our routine, we achieved more consistent sleeping patterns.

Though challenging, prioritizing sleep proved to be one of the best decisions for our family. It taught us the importance of self-care in parenting. A well-rested parent, we learned, is better equipped to provide care.

Devise a Feeding Plan

Consult with your healthcare provider to establish a feeding schedule tailored to your baby's needs. Preterm babies often require more frequent feedings and may struggle with latching or sucking, so patience and persistence are key. If breastfeeding proves challenging, seek guidance and support from a lactation consultant.

Our journey to establish a feeding routine for our preterm baby was indeed challenging, but it was integral for his growth and development. Initially, we started with cup and spoon feeding under the guidance of nurses in the NICU. As the mother was still recovering in ICU, expressing breast milk and feeding our baby was the only option. After leaving the ICU, the mother continued to express breast milk, and we also introduced our baby to direct breastfeeding.

We experimented with different feeding positions and techniques to ensure proper latching and an adequate milk supply. We also maintained a feeding log, noting feeding times, durations, and the number of wet and dirty diapers to monitor hydration and intake.

Feeding a preterm baby often tests your patience, as they may have trouble latching or sucking. Thus, we allowed breaks during feedings and tried various positions for our baby's comfort.

Additionally, administering multivitamins and medication posed a new set of challenges as our baby did not prefer the taste. One helpful approach was mixing the medicine or multivitamins with breast milk to make it more palatable. Following the doctor's instructions and communicating any concerns or issues to the healthcare provider is essential.

Ultimately, developing a feeding routine for our preterm baby was a process of trial and error, requiring open communication with our healthcare providers and a lactation consultant. Patience and persistence led us to a routine that ensured our baby's growth and well-being.

Seek Professional Help

If you're dealing with colic or other issues, don't hesitate to consult a healthcare professional. They can provide strategies to soothe a colicky baby, such as swaddling, using white noise, or offering a pacifier.

Preterm babies often require specialized care, and healthcare professionals are trained to provide this care. They can guide you on issues like feeding difficulties, weight gain, respiratory problems, or even emotional challenges as a parent of a preterm baby.

When our baby suffered from colic, we initially tried various strategies, from lullabies to gentle rocking, but to no avail. Our pediatrician recommended swaddling our baby tightly and using white noise as a soothing background, both of which had a calming effect on our baby.

The experience reinforced the importance of parental self-care, especially when dealing with a colicky baby. Our pediatrician emphasized taking breaks and seeking support from loved ones.

Reaching out to a healthcare professional provided strategies to soothe our colicky baby and equipped us with the resources to be more confident parents. If you're facing difficulties with your preterm baby, seeking professional guidance is highly recommended.

Share Responsibilities

Caring for a preterm baby can be physically and emotionally taxing, so both parents must share the responsibilities. This can involve dividing tasks such as feeding, changing diapers, soothing the baby, and taking turns attending to the baby at night.

In our experience, we learned that teamwork and shared responsibility were key in managing the care of our preterm baby while also considering our individual physical and emotional well-being. Feeding, an essential aspect of newborn care, became a shared endeavor. As my wife handled breastfeeding, I assisted with milk expression and ensuring proper positioning and latching for feedings.

We are also both engaged in KMC, a skin-to-skin contact method that promotes bonding, helps regulate the baby's physiological processes, and supports breastfeeding. This practice is beneficial for the baby and provides a chance for both of us to bond with him.

In addition to feeding and KMC, we divided tasks such as changing diapers, bathing the baby, and comforting him when upset. We alternated night duties, allowing each other to rest. I took up additional household chores to ease the load on my wife.

Communication was vital in this process; we kept each other in the loop about our feelings, concerns, and needs. We visited the health facility for regular check-ups and reviews and maintained a log of our baby's growth and weight milestones. Financial, emotional, and spiritual support were integral to our shared responsibilities, and working as a team, we ensured the best care for our baby.

Take Care of Yourself

Parents must prioritize their physical and emotional well-being to best care for their preterm baby. This can involve getting adequate sleep, maintaining a healthy diet, and setting aside time for relaxation. Counseling or therapy may also be considered to help address any emotional issues associated with caring for a preterm baby.

Educate Yourselves

Gaining as much knowledge as possible about caring for a preterm baby can help parents feel more confident and prepared. This can involve attending classes or workshops on preterm baby care, seeking advice and guidance from the baby's healthcare team, or reading literature on the subject.

Education was a vital part of our preparation for our preterm baby. We attended classes and workshops on preterm baby care and engaged extensively with our healthcare team. Reading about others' experiences in books and articles on preterm baby care also gave us much-needed perspective and made us feel less alone.

We also found great support from other parents of preterm babies. Connecting with them through online support groups and local organizations allowed us to share our concerns, ask questions, and receive empathetic support. Our continuous learning journey made us feel more confident and equipped to care for our baby.

Nurturing and Nutrition of a Preterm Infant:

The task of nurturing a preterm baby entails extra responsibilities. For both parents to evenly distribute the burden and sustain a robust relationship, consider the following tactics:

Keep an open dialogue: Share your anxieties, sentiments, and necessities with your spouse to ensure mutual understanding. Frequent dialogues can help prevent miscommunication and confirm shared expectations.

Feeding a preterm infant necessitates specific care to meet their dietary requirements. Here are some tactics to help parents improve proper nourishment for their preterm infant:

Please seek advice from healthcare professionals: It is crucial to confer with a healthcare expert, such as a neonatologist, pediatrician, or lactation consultant, to devise a feeding regimen suited to your infant's unique needs. They can guide you regarding the appropriate feeding timeline, quantity of milk or formula required, and any necessary supplements.

Promote breast milk use: Breast milk holds significant value for preterm babies since it offers them the best nutrition and immunity against diseases. In our situation, our healthcare provider advised us to feed our baby breast milk exclusively. Although his small size made initial breastfeeding attempts challenging, with the assistance of a lactation counselor and our healthcare provider, we found the right positioning and technique to facilitate breastfeeding.

Besides direct breastfeeding, we also expressed breast milk for our baby, which was then administered to him via a cup and spoon. Our healthcare provider gave us precise instructions about preparing and storing the breast milk to ensure its safety for our baby's consumption. We carefully followed these directions to mitigate any contamination or spoilage risks.

We ensured regular pumping sessions to sustain a healthy milk supply for our baby. While pumping and expressing breast milk every few hours can be exhausting, ensuring a continuous milk supply for the baby is crucial.

In case breastfeeding or milk expression is not viable, consult your healthcare provider about other alternatives like donor milk or formula specially designed for preterm babies. Always check with your healthcare provider to establish the best feeding regimen for your preterm baby.

Embrace kangaroo care: We strongly recommend practicing kangaroo care for anyone nurturing a preterm baby. Kangaroo care entails holding the baby skin-to-skin on the parent's chest. This practice improved our baby's breastfeeding ability and even augmented milk production.

Kangaroo care aids breast milk production because when the baby is held close to the parent's chest, it can stimulate the hormones responsible for producing breast milk. After we practiced kangaroo care, we noticed an increased frequency and duration of our baby's breastfeeding sessions. This amplified the milk supply, which is crucial for our baby's growth and development.

Besides benefiting from breastfeeding and milk production, kangaroo care also facilitated our bonding with our baby. The skin-to-skin contact offered comfort and warmth, which was especially important since our baby was born preterm and spent time in the NICU. It established a connection with him and provided him with a sense of comfort and security.

Practicing kangaroo care emerged as one of the most beneficial strategies for nurturing preterm babies. Not only did it aid with breastfeeding and milk production, but it also provided invaluable opportunities for bonding and comfort. We highly endorse it for other parents of preterm babies.

Contemplate feeding tubes: While our baby was fully developed and didn't need feeding tubes, not all preterm babies are the same. If the baby is unable to suckle or swallow efficiently, feeding tubes may be necessary to ensure they receive adequate nutrition. This may be temporary until the baby can breastfeed or feed with a cup and spoon. In some instances, the baby may not have developed the reflexes necessary to suck and swallow, or they may be too weak to ingest sufficient nutrition. In such situations, a feeding tube can be a temporary solution until the baby matures and can feed independently.

Feeding tubes do not preclude the possibility of breastfeeding. In many cases, the baby may still be able to breastfeed while receiving additional nutrition via the feeding tube. This can be a gradual process, with the baby incrementally consuming more feed orally as they gain strength and ability.

Work closely with the baby's healthcare team to ensure proper feeding tube use and confirm the baby's adequate nutrition. The healthcare team will monitor the baby's growth and development and adjust the feeding plan as necessary. Discuss any worries or queries with the healthcare team, as they can provide guidance and support, ensuring the baby receives optimal care.

Monitor weight gain: Preterm babies may need more frequent weight checks to monitor their weight gain and confirm they receive sufficient nutrition.

For our preterm baby, tracking his weight gain was critical to his care. Our healthcare provider advised us on the appropriate frequency of weigh-ins, which for us was monthly. We found that monitoring our baby's weight ensured he was adequately nourished and motivated us as parents, especially for the mother.

With our baby being born underweight, every gram he gained was a reason to celebrate. We eagerly anticipated his monthly weigh-ins and cheered him on as we watched the scale numbers increase. Observing him grow and thrive was reassuring, giving us a sense of achievement as parents.

In addition to weight monitoring, we tracked other growth milestones like head circumference and length. This kept us updated about our baby's development and alerted us to potential medical issues. Acquiring a child health card and plotting the baby's weight from birth is essential for proper weight gain monitoring. This will allow tracking of the baby's growth and development over time and confirm that they are meeting their milestones. It's also a valuable tool for healthcare providers to assess your baby's health and development during regular check-ups.

We advise other parents of preterm babies to work closely with their healthcare provider to track their weight gain and growth milestones. This can serve as a source of motivation and a means of staying informed about their baby's health and development.

Implement pace feeding: Preterm babies may quickly tire during feedings, so pacing the feeding by taking breaks and burping the baby can help them conserve energy and prevent overfeeding. Given their small size and underdeveloped muscles, ensuring they don't exhaust themselves while eating is vital. One technique to pace the feeding is to pause and burp the baby during the feeding process. This can help the baby conserve energy and prevent overfeeding.

Remember that preterm babies may have a weaker suck, so it's essential to feed them slowly and patiently. Also, preterm babies may need more diminutive and frequent feeds than full-term babies, so working with a healthcare professional to establish a suitable feeding schedule is vital.

When we introduced paced feeding to our preterm baby, we found that taking breaks and burping him during feedings helped him conserve energy and prevent fatigue. We also collaborated with our healthcare professional to set a feeding schedule for our baby that involved smaller and more frequent feeding. By implementing these techniques, we were able to help our preterm baby grow and develop at a healthy pace.

CHAPTER 7

ᘒᘒᘒᘒᘒ

CHALLENGES OF HAVING A PRETERM BABY

Parenthood is a journey like no other, filled with joy, love, and boundless wonder. But when your baby is born preterm, the journey can take an unexpected and sometimes challenging turn. This chapter provides you, the parents, with a detailed guide to navigating the hurdles of having a preterm baby. The arrival of a preterm baby can feel daunting, but armed with the proper knowledge, strategies, and support, you can navigate these waters with certainty and care.

Ranging from common conditions like jaundice and colic to issues like low birth weight, eating challenges, and other potential health complications, the world of a preterm baby may seem filled with endless challenges. However, each can be overcome or managed effectively with the right approach, attitude, and tools.

Our aim is to inform and instill confidence in your abilities as a parent and/or caregiver. The journey with your preterm baby will require strength, patience, and resilience, and we're here to ensure that you feel equipped and prepared. By exploring practical solutions, sharing personal experiences, and offering resources for emotional support, we hope to transform these challenges into milestones of your shared journey.

Ultimately, we hope this knowledge will empower you to fully embrace your role and provide the best care and love for your preterm baby. So, let's begin this journey together, step by step, meeting each challenge head-on with courage and understanding.

Jaundice in Preterm Babies

One of the most common conditions encountered with newborns, especially preterm babies, is jaundice. It manifests as a distinct yellowish discoloration of the skin and the whites of the eyes, lending the condition its name, derived from the French word 'jaune,' meaning 'yellow.'

Jaundice arises due to high levels of bilirubin, a waste product produced by the body during the normal process of breaking down old red blood cells. Ordinarily, the liver plays a vital role in processing and removing bilirubin from the body. However, in preterm babies, the liver might not fully develop, making it difficult to break down bilirubin effectively. This causes bilirubin to build up in the baby's body, leading to jaundice.

The relatively high incidence of jaundice among preterm babies is primarily a consequence of their immature liver and increased bilirubin production. Their red blood cells have a shorter lifespan, leading to a higher rate of bilirubin production, and their liver lacks the total capacity to eliminate bilirubin from the body effectively.

Understanding the cause of jaundice is the first step towards managing it. In the following sections, we will discuss strategies for dealing with jaundice and methods to support your preterm baby's liver in handling bilirubin. It's essential to remember that jaundice in newborns, although familiar (about 3 in 5 newborns), can have serious implications if not addressed promptly and appropriately, underlining the importance of healthcare professionals' guidance in managing this condition.

Strategies for Managing Jaundice

When dealing with jaundice in preterm babies, parents can implement several strategies, both at home and with the aid of medical professionals. It's important to note that any approach to managing jaundice should be under the guidance of a pediatrician or healthcare provider. Here are some strategies:

Sunlight Exposure: Natural sunlight is a simple and effective way to help reduce bilirubin levels in a baby's body. When the baby's skin is exposed to sunlight, the light alters the bilirubin in the baby's blood into a form that can be more easily processed and eliminated by the immature liver. It's important to remember, however, that newborns have susceptible skin, so sunlight exposure should be limited to early morning or late afternoon hours to avoid harsh sunlight. Also, avoid exposing the baby directly to the sun; let sunlight come through a window to reduce the risk of sunburn.

Medical Interventions: While moderate sunlight exposure can help, many preterm babies with jaundice may require additional medical interventions. These can include:

Phototherapy is the most common treatment for newborn jaundice: In this process, the baby is placed under a particular type of light (not sunlight) that emits light in the blue-green spectrum. This light changes the shape and structure of the bilirubin molecules in the baby's body, allowing them to be excreted in the urine and stool. The baby's eyes are covered to protect them during this treatment.

Intravenous Immunoglobulin (IVIG): IVIG can be used if the baby's jaundice is caused by blood type incompatibility between the mother and the baby. This treatment involves infusing the baby with antibodies to lower the levels of antibodies from the mother, which breaks down the baby's red blood cells.

Exchange Transfusion: In severe cases of jaundice, if the bilirubin levels are incredibly high and pose a risk of brain damage, an exchange transfusion might be necessary. This process involves rapidly replacing the baby's blood with donor blood to lower bilirubin levels.

However, every preterm baby's situation is unique, and the treatment plan will vary depending on the baby's bilirubin levels and overall health condition. Regular follow-ups with the pediatrician and strict adherence to their advice are crucial in managing jaundice effectively in preterm babies.

Personal Experience with Jaundice in Preterm Babies

In our case, we were fortunate that our preterm baby did not develop jaundice. From the early stages, our healthcare providers were vigilant and proactive in their efforts to ensure that our baby's liver function was adequately boosted. Their interventions, along with regular monitoring of his bilirubin levels, allowed us to avoid the experience of managing jaundice in our baby.

However, we understand that this isn't the case for all parents of preterm babies. We've met and spoken with other parents in support groups and hospital settings who have had to deal with this challenge. These interactions allowed us to see first-hand the fear and anxiety that can come with a jaundice diagnosis in a preterm baby, but also the relief and happiness when the bilirubin levels finally start to decrease.

One critical insight from our conversations with other parents was the importance of awareness and timely intervention. Knowing what to look for - the tell-tale yellowing of the skin and eyes - and when to seek medical advice can make a big difference in managing jaundice. Moreover, we saw the benefits of following the pediatrician's advice, whether that involved sunlight exposure or more intensive treatments like phototherapy.

While we did not experience jaundice with our preterm baby, these experiences underscored for us the challenges that preterm babies and their parents may have to face. It reaffirmed our belief in the importance of knowledge, support, and appropriate medical care in dealing with these challenges.

Colic in Preterm Babies

Colic is a condition commonly found in newborns, and even more so in preterm babies. It's characterized by excessive, often intense crying that may seem to have no apparent cause. While all babies cry, colicky babies cry more than others, frequently in the late afternoon or evening. The crying often goes on for three or more hours a day, three or more days a week, for three or more weeks.

Although the exact cause of colic is still somewhat of a mystery, it is believed that it may be linked to the immaturity of a baby's digestive system. Preterm babies, whose systems are even less developed, are therefore more susceptible to suffering from this condition.

The signs of colic can be distressing to witness. Babies may cry intensely, clench their fists, arch their backs, and even go red in the face. They may also show signs of gastrointestinal discomfort, like passing gas more than other babies and having a bloated tummy.

It's important to note that colic is quite common. While it can be highly stressful and exhausting, it usually doesn't have any long-term effects on a baby's health. It typically starts a few weeks after birth and improves significantly when the baby is 3 to 4 months old. However, for parents of preterm babies who are already dealing with various other challenges, colic can add an extra layer of worry and exhaustion.

While it is challenging to manage, knowing what colic is, understanding that it is temporary, and learning about how to soothe a colicky baby can make this period more bearable for parents.

Home Remedies and Medical Advice for Managing Colic

Soothing a colicky baby can sometimes feel like an uphill battle, but there are several strategies that parents can try. These include:

Gentle Rocking: Holding your baby and gently rocking it can be comforting. Some parents find that baby slings or carriers can help keep their hands free while providing the soothing motion babies crave.

Swaddling: Swaddling mimics the snug environment of the womb and can be calming for babies. Be sure to swaddle your baby correctly, ensuring their hips can move and aren't overheated.

White Noise: Many babies find white noise soothing. This could be the sound of a vacuum cleaner, a fan, or white noise from a smartphone app. The noise mimics the sounds they'd hear in the womb.

Warm Bath: A warm bath can be soothing if your baby enjoys bath time. Always check the water temperature, and never leave your baby unattended in the tub.

Massage: Gentle tummy massages can help to relieve gas, which could be contributing to your baby's discomfort.

Remember that while these home remedies can be effective, they may not work for every baby, and that's okay. Consulting with a healthcare provider is a good idea if your baby's crying persists or seems particularly intense. They can rule out other possible medical causes of excessive crying and provide additional strategies for managing colic.

Keeping a detailed record of your baby's crying patterns can be helpful for both you and your pediatrician. Note when the crying happens, how long it lasts, and anything that seems to trigger or calm it down. This information can help your healthcare provider to understand your baby's symptoms better and make more personalized recommendations.

Personal Experience with Colic in Preterm Babies

Our experience with colic and our preterm baby was one of the most challenging parts of our early parenthood journey. Our little one cried for what seemed like hours, especially in the late afternoon and evening, and it often seemed like there was nothing we could do to console him.

The sight of our baby in pain and crying was heart-wrenching. We felt helpless and worried, which I believe are feelings common among parents dealing with a colicky baby.

However, we didn't lose hope. We tried various home remedies, including swaddling, white noise, and warm baths, but gentle rocking was the most effective. I remember many nights of slow dancing around the living room, humming soft lullabies as our baby finally found peace in the rhythm and warmth of our movements. We did after spending quite some amount of money buying pharmaceutical remedies, including colic gripe water, which seems ineffective in soothing it. We also outrightly rejected advice to give our preterm all kinds of traditional remedies, such as local herbs, as we weren't sure about their safety.

In addition, we meticulously recorded our baby's crying spells, noting the time of day, the length of crying, and any potential triggers we noticed. We shared this information with our pediatrician, who helped us better understand the nature and pattern of colic.

The experience taught us patience and resilience, and with time, our baby's colic episodes gradually reduced. It's important to remember that colic doesn't last forever, and getting through this challenging time requires a lot of support, patience, and self-care. Contact your healthcare providers and lean on your support system; you're not alone. We needed to prepare for the night by having daytime rest so that we could accommodate the colic of our baby. We often soothed him during the evening, especially when the crying was too intense.

Low Birth Weight in Preterm Babies

Preterm babies often have low birth weight, a consequence of not having had enough time to grow and develop in the womb. Being born too early can limit a baby's growth, resulting in them weighing significantly less than their full-term counterparts at birth.

Low birth weight can present several challenges, including difficulties with feeding and maintaining body temperature, as well as an increased risk for infections and long-term developmental problems. It's essential to understand that low birth weight is a common issue for preterm babies, but with the proper care and medical attention, these babies can grow and thrive just like any other child.

It's important to remember that each preterm baby is unique and may grow at their own pace. Therefore, their weight gain may be slower compared to full-term babies. Regular growth monitoring and pediatric consultations are vital to ensure your baby is growing healthily.

While dealing with low birth weight can be emotionally taxing, remember that it's a journey. Celebrate every ounce gained and each small victory along the way. While the path may seem slow and steady, with patience and the right attitude and support, your preterm baby can overcome the challenges associated with low birth weight.

Monitoring Baby's Weight Gain and Seeking Medical Attention

Tracking your preterm baby's weight gain is critical to ensuring healthy growth and development. Regular weight checks during pediatrician visits will help monitor this growth over time. In between visits, you might also be advised to maintain a growth chart at home, tracking the baby's weight and other growth parameters.

Because preterm babies often grow slower than their full-term counterparts, it's important not to compare your baby's weight gain to that of a full-term baby. Instead, your pediatrician will use specific growth charts designed for preterm infants, which take into account their unique growth patterns.

While some weight fluctuation is normal, especially in the first few days after birth, consistent weight loss or a lack of weight gain over time can be cause for concern. Other signs that may indicate a problem include:

- ❖ Changes in eating habits, such as showing less interest in feedings or struggling to latch or suck.

- ❖ Fewer wet or dirty diapers, indicating that the baby may not be getting enough nourishment.

- ❖ Changes in energy level and responsiveness.

- ❖ Unexplained irritability or fussiness.

- ❖ A drop in the baby's body temperature.

If you notice any of these signs or are worried about your baby's weight gain, it's essential to seek medical attention promptly. A healthcare provider can assess your baby's overall health and development, adjust their feeding plan if necessary, and provide guidance and reassurance to help you navigate this phase.

The Role of Regular Pediatric Check-Ups in Ensuring Healthy Progress

Regular pediatric check-ups are indispensable in ensuring your preterm baby's healthy progress. These visits focus on the physical aspects of growth, such as weight gain, and monitor the development of crucial cognitive and motor skills.

Tracking Growth: Regular measurements of your baby's weight, length, and head circumference provide valuable insight into their growth and development. These measurements are plotted on a growth chart designed for preterm babies to track their progress over time.

Developmental Screening: These check-ups also evaluate your baby's development in various areas, such as cognitive, motor, speech, and social-emotional skills. This screening helps to detect potential developmental delays early, enabling timely intervention and support.

Vaccinations: Regular pediatric visits ensure that your preterm baby receives all necessary vaccinations as per their adjusted age. Vaccines are crucial for protecting your baby from various preventable diseases.

Nutrition Guidance: Pediatricians and Nutritionists provide personalized guidance on feeding and nutrition based on your baby's unique needs. This advice can be particularly beneficial for preterm babies who often struggle with feeding.

Parental Support and Education: These check-ups offer an opportunity to ask questions, express concerns, and learn more about your baby's care and development. They offer reassurance and guidance to parents navigating the challenging journey of raising a preterm baby.

Regular pediatric check-ups are essential for tracking your preterm baby's health and development, spotting potential issues early, and providing the best care possible.

Why Feeding a Preterm Baby Can Be Challenging

Feeding a preterm baby can be a challenging task for new parents. The difficulties primarily arise from the baby's underdeveloped reflexes and physical strength, unique nutritional needs, and potential health complications. Here are some reasons why feeding a preterm baby can be challenging:

Immature Sucking and Swallowing Reflexes: A baby's ability to suck and swallow is often not fully developed until around 34 weeks of gestation. Babies born before this time may not yet have the coordination to suck, swallow, and breathe in the correct order, making feeding sessions complicated and exhausting.

Underdeveloped Digestive System: A preterm baby's digestive system is not fully mature, making it harder to digest breast milk or formula. They may have difficulty absorbing nutrients or may suffer from digestive problems such as gastroesophageal reflux disease (GERD).

Respiratory Issues: Many preterm babies suffer from respiratory conditions such as bronchopulmonary dysplasia (BPD) or respiratory distress syndrome (RDS). These conditions can make it hard for the baby to breathe and feed simultaneously.

Unique Nutritional Needs: Preterm babies have unique nutritional needs. They require more calories, protein, and certain micronutrients to catch up on growth than full-term babies. Balancing these nutritional needs can be a delicate task.

Oral Aversion: Some preterm babies develop an aversion to oral feeding, especially those with medical procedures involving their mouth or throat. This can make them resist feeding, leading to further complications.

Understanding these challenges can help parents approach feeding their preterm baby with patience and empathy. Each baby is unique, and what works for one may not work for another. It's essential to work closely with healthcare professionals to develop a feeding plan that best meets the needs of your preterm baby.

Techniques to Improve Feeding Experiences

Feeding a preterm baby requires patience, practice, and plenty of time. Here are some techniques that can improve feeding experiences:

Different Feeding Positions: Experiment with different feeding positions to find one that is comfortable for both you and your baby. The semi-upright position can be useful, especially for preterm babies with a high reflux risk. In this position, you hold your baby seated in your lap, supporting the baby's head and neck.

Specialized Bottles and Nipples: Bottles and nipples are explicitly designed for preterm or low-birth-weight babies. These products are typically easy to handle and designed to reduce the air the baby swallows, which can help minimize gas and discomfort. However, only use these under the guidance of your medical and nutrition care teams.

Paced Bottle Feeding: This feeding method lets the baby control the milk flow, mimicking the breastfeeding experience. It involves holding the bottle horizontally and allowing the baby to "latch" onto the nipple. The baby then regulates the pace of the feeding by sucking when they're ready. Only use bottle feeding under the guidance of your medical and nutrition care teams to avoid the risk of diarrhea and other infections.

Skin-to-Skin Contact: Also known as Kangaroo Care, this technique involves holding the baby against your skin. It can calm your baby, regulate their heart rate and breathing, and stimulate their interest in feeding.

Support from a Lactation Consultant: A lactation consultant can provide valuable advice and hands-on assistance to help you navigate the challenges of feeding a preterm baby. They can demonstrate different feeding positions, help ensure the baby is latching correctly, and provide guidance on expressing and storing milk.

Remember, it's okay if feeding your preterm baby seems challenging at first. With time, you and your baby will develop a routine that works for both of you. Always communicate with your healthcare team about any concerns or issues during feeding. They can provide additional guidance and reassurance.

The Importance of Acknowledging and Managing Emotional Stress Associated with Feeding Challenges:

Feeding challenges with a preterm baby can elicit a range of emotions from parents and caregivers. Feelings of frustration, sadness, guilt, anxiety, or even failure are common responses. These emotions can be overwhelming and, if left unchecked, can contribute to emotional distress or even postnatal depression. Acknowledging and managing these feelings is as vital as addressing the physical aspects of feeding challenges.

Acknowledging Your Feelings: The first step is acknowledging your feelings. You might feel frustrated if feeding isn't going as planned or guilty that you're not providing for your baby in the way you'd hoped. These feelings are entirely normal, and acknowledging them allows you to begin processing and managing them.

Practicing Self-Care: Caring for a preterm baby can be demanding, and neglecting your own needs is easy. However, self-care is vital during this time. Ensure you're eating well, getting as much rest as possible, and taking breaks when you can. This could be as simple as taking a few minutes to read a book, enjoy a cup of tea, or take a short walk outside.

Seeking Support: Reach out to others for support, whether it's your spouse, family, friends, or healthcare professionals. Don't hesitate to express your feelings and ask for help when needed. Speaking with others who've had similar experiences can be comforting and provide practical advice and reassurance. You may also find comfort in your spiritual circles through fellowship, simply taking time to read your Holy Book, or praying.

Professional Help: If distress persists, seeking help from a mental health professional is essential. Therapists or counselors, particularly those specializing in postnatal issues, can provide strategies to manage stress and deal with the emotional challenges of caring for a preterm baby.

Remember, it's okay to find this time challenging and to ask for help. Navigating the journey of feeding a preterm baby is not something you have to do alone. With support, every step, even the challenging ones, will become a milestone in your unique parenting journey.

We had bits and pieces of the above recommendations, which worked well for us. We primarily worked closely with our friends, Church and home cell members, and professional healthcare providers who supported us in each step of the journey. The good news for us is we had a nearby medical facility, Nutritionists, and spiritual leaders whom we relied on most of the time. We understand this may not always be the case for all other parents and caregivers of preterm babies. We encourage you to consider what works best for your unique situation.

Overview of Potential Health Challenges: Respiratory Issues, Infections, Developmental Delays

Preterm babies, due to their premature entry into the world, are often at risk of various health challenges. Understanding these potential complications can better equip parents to support their baby's health and development. Below, we highlight some of the common health challenges faced by preterm babies:

Respiratory Issues: The lungs are one of the last organs to mature in the womb, so preterm babies often experience respiratory complications. These can range from mild issues like rapid breathing (tachypnoea) to more severe conditions like Respiratory Distress Syndrome (RDS) or Bronchopulmonary Dysplasia (BPD).

Infections: Preterm babies have underdeveloped immune systems, making them more vulnerable to infections. These can include common newborn infections like pneumonia and meningitis and less common but more severe infections like sepsis.

Developmental Delays: Preterm babies might face developmental delays in physical, cognitive, or behavioral growth. Early intervention services are often recommended to support and monitor the baby's progress, helping to identify and address potential delays as soon as possible.

Other Health Challenges

Preterm babies may also face different health challenges, such as difficulty maintaining body temperature, anemia, or problems with hearing and vision. Regular check-ups and screenings are essential to monitor these potential issues and ensure appropriate interventions when necessary.

Caring for a preterm baby with health challenges can be demanding, but remember, every baby's journey is unique, and progress isn't always linear. As parents, your love, care, patience, and persistence will support your baby's growth and development. And while these challenges might seem daunting, with the proper care and support, most preterm babies grow to be healthy children and adults.

The Importance of Working with Healthcare Providers to Address Challenges and Create Individualized Care Plans

The journey of parenting a preterm baby can be challenging, and it's essential to work closely with your healthcare providers to navigate these challenges. Your baby's doctors, nurses, nutritionists, therapists, and other healthcare professionals will be integral members of your baby's care team. Here's why working closely with them is crucial:

Creating Individualized Care Plans: Every preterm baby is unique and might encounter different health challenges. Healthcare providers can help create an individualized care plan tailored to meet your baby's specific needs and optimize their health and development. This plan may encompass medical treatments, therapies, nutrition plans, and home care strategies.

Addressing Health Challenges: Preterm babies often have an increased risk of health complications like respiratory issues, infections, and developmental delays. Working closely with your healthcare providers enables early detection and prompt treatment of these potential problems. Timely intervention can significantly impact your baby's recovery and overall development.

Monitoring Progress: Regular check-ups with healthcare providers are crucial to monitor your baby's growth and development and adjust the care plan as necessary. These visits are opportunities to discuss your concerns, observe progress, and get reassurance about your baby's health status.

Support and Guidance: Healthcare providers can offer invaluable support and guidance beyond providing medical care. They can help alleviate your anxieties, equip you with necessary skills (like CPR or feeding techniques), and guide you to additional resources, such as support groups or specialized therapies.

Remember, while you may feel overwhelmed sometimes, you are not alone. Your healthcare team's combined expertise and support, along with your love and care as parents, are the key ingredients in nurturing your preterm baby to good health and development.

Early Intervention Services and Therapy

Early intervention services play a crucial role in the development of preterm babies facing potential health challenges. These services comprise a coordinated effort system designed to address developmental and health issues as early as possible. By providing these interventions at an early stage, they help minimize the impact of these problems and enhance the baby's development. Early intervention services can include:

Physical Therapy: Physical therapy can be invaluable for preterm babies facing muscle development and motor skills challenges. Physical therapists work to improve strength, coordination, and balance, setting a foundation for crawling, walking, and other movement skills.

Occupational Therapy: Occupational therapists help children develop skills necessary for daily activities. This could include assisting with feeding challenges, fostering hand-eye coordination, or helping a child learn to self-soothe.

Speech and Language Therapy: If a preterm baby shows signs of delayed speech or difficulties with swallowing, a speech and language therapist can provide targeted interventions to improve these skills.

Developmental Services: Some early intervention programs offer general developmental services. These comprehensive programs work on cognitive, social, and emotional development alongside physical growth and skills.

Parental Training: Early intervention isn't just for babies; it also includes training and resources for parents. This can help you better understand your baby's needs, equip you with strategies to handle different challenges and guide you in promoting your baby's development at home.

Professionals collaborating to address the child's needs typically provide early intervention services. The family's involvement is a crucial component of these programs, and as a parent, your role in your baby's development is paramount. These services can make a significant difference, providing your baby with the best start and setting the stage for long-term success.

Conclusion

Having a preterm baby is indeed a challenging journey that can feel overwhelming. However, with knowledge and understanding about these unique challenges ranging from jaundice, colic, low birth weight, and feeding difficulties to broader health issues, parents can feel more prepared and empowered.

It's important to remember that every child's journey is different, and what works for one may not work for another. Parents should always feel comfortable seeking advice from healthcare providers and utilizing resources such as lactation consultants or early intervention services.

Through our journey with a preterm baby, we have come to appreciate the strength and resilience of these little fighters. While the early days are fraught with challenges and concerns, it's crucial to remember that most preterm babies grow into healthy children and adults.

This chapter aimed to provide insight into the challenges of a preterm baby and some strategies for handling them. Always keep in mind that you're not alone on this journey. A wealth of professional help is available, as is a community of parents who have experienced similar circumstances. Ultimately, love, patience, and care go a long way in helping your preterm baby grow and thrive.

CHAPTER 8

⋘⋘⋘⋘⋘

FINDING YOUR FEET

Bringing my first baby home was a whirlwind of emotions and adjustments. Suddenly, my daily routine was no longer my own; it revolved around this tiny, beautiful being who arrived earlier than expected. My social life transformed as I prioritized my baby's needs over coffee dates and gatherings.

Most significantly, my relationships evolved. With my spouse, we navigated this new world of parenthood together, sometimes clumsily but always with love. My family, too, became an invaluable source of support, offering help and understanding in ways I hadn't anticipated. Through all these changes, I was not just finding my feet but discovering a new, profound sense of purpose and identity.

In this chapter, we will start with how to use your feet as a mother.

Finding Your Feet as a Mother

The transition to motherhood, especially with a preterm baby, is a profound journey that reshapes every aspect of life. This phase often brings a sense of awe and overwhelming responsibility. Suddenly, your priorities shift entirely toward the care and well-being of your child.

This section delves into the myriad emotions and changes you encounter from the initial shock and adjustment to the gradual embrace of your new role. It's a time of self-discovery, where you learn the depths of your strength and resilience. You begin to see the world through the lens of a mother, a perspective that is both challenging and immensely rewarding.

This journey is not just about nurturing your child; it's also about encouraging your growth, discovering new facets of your identity, and embracing the profound transformation that motherhood brings.

Embracing the New Dawn

Becoming a mother, particularly to a preterm baby, is a journey marked by a spectrum of profound emotions, significant physical changes, and complex social adjustments. This part of our narrative explores this transformation's diverse and intricate aspects. It's a path that intertwines vulnerability with strength, uncertainty with discovery, and challenges with triumphs.

As we unfold the layers of this experience, we shed light on the emotional roller coaster, the resilience required for physical recovery, and the evolution of relationships. It's a testament to the power of motherhood in reshaping life's priorities, perspectives, and personal identity. This section serves as a guide and a companion, offering understanding, support, and insight into the remarkable journey of becoming a mother under extraordinary circumstances.

After the birth of a preterm baby, a mother's body embarks on a journey of recovery that is both physical and emotional. This recovery is not just about healing from childbirth but also adapting to the preterm nature of the delivery. I experienced a range of physical sensations, from exhaustion to physical discomfort, that were both expected and surprising. Ours was explicitly more complex as our baby was delivered through C-section due to pre-eclampsia-related complications.

My spouse spent two days in the intensive care unit (ICU) under the observation of medical care teams to control the high blood pressure. The physical pain from the wound of the C-section, coupled with the emotional exhaustion of the preterm birth and being separated from your newborn baby, had a heavy toll on her. Our preterm was placed in the neonatal ICU, away from the mother.

Even after discharge from the ICU, I could see how much physical pain she bore. Observing her in that state caused me pain as well. So, we journeyed together while reassuring each other that it would be alright.

The demands of caring for a fragile newborn, coupled with the healing process, required a delicate balance. This started in the hospital, where the mother had to learn to adjust her sleeping posture to accommodate our new jewel. It wasn't always comfortable, but we embraced the changes with joy and love.

I learned the importance of nutrition, which was crucial to my recovery and well-being. I should confess I was never a person who cared much about what we ate before giving birth to our first baby. The fact that we had a preterm and low birth weight baby who depended on my ability to breastfeed him for rapid weight gain adequately meant I had to adjust my eating habits religiously. I even started eating diverse vegetables and fruits and drinking plenty of water.

Eating healthily was about my health and providing the best for our baby, significantly helping produce adequate breast milk. Rest, though hard to come by with a newborn, became a vital component of my recovery. I had to learn to take moments of rest whenever possible, understanding that it was crucial for her physical and mental recovery.

Physical therapy or gentle exercises were recommended to me to help strengthen my body. These exercises were not just about fitness but about reconnecting with and reclaiming my body after the experience of preterm childbirth. The changes in my body, some temporary and some permanent, were a testament to my journey. For instance, I had to put up with a permanent C-section scar, which will forever remind me of the birth of our first baby.

Regular check-ups with my healthcare provider were crucial. They monitored my physical recovery and provided support for navigating this new phase of life. During these check-ups, I could discuss any concerns or symptoms, no matter how small they seemed.

The psychological impact of these physical changes was significant. There were moments of self-doubt and anxiety about my body's ability to recover. But, with time, I learned to appreciate and respect my body's resilience and the incredible journey it had gone through. This part of my story is not just about healing my body but also about the growth of my spirit and the deepening of my understanding of motherhood.

This content aims to provide a detailed and empathetic perspective on the physical and emotional journey of recovery after preterm birth, offering support and understanding to new mothers undergoing this experience.

Heartstrings of Change

Understanding the emotional terrain of new motherhood, particularly after preterm birth, has been a journey of profound shifts and discoveries for me. This experience illuminated a mother's complex web of emotions as she stepped into her new role. Joy, anxiety, love, and fear became constant companions, often coexisting in unexpected ways.

There were moments of feeling inadequate, yet they were coupled with an overwhelming love for my child. In this section, I share my experiences and the coping strategies I learned, emphasizing the importance of emotional support and nurturing mental well-being.

This journey has not only been about adapting to a new role but also about understanding and embracing the psychological transformation that accompanies it. As I held my preterm baby for the first time, a surge of emotions overwhelmed me. The depth of love I felt was profound yet intermingled with an acute fear for this tiny, delicate life in my arms. In those early days, the joy of motherhood was often shadowed by guilt for not having a full-term pregnancy and for the challenges my baby faced. But with each small milestone, a wave of relief and happiness washed over me, reminding me of our incredible journey.

As I nursed or watched over my baby in the stillness of the night, I found myself lost in thought. Hope and fear coexisted in my heart, each vying for dominance. These moments, though solitary, were also when I felt the strongest connection to my child. They were times of introspection, where I learned the true meaning of resilience and unconditional love.

The isolation of early motherhood, especially under such unique circumstances, was palpable. Yet, I found solace in the stories of other mothers who had walked this path before me. Their experiences, shared in quiet conversations or support group meetings, brought a sense of community and understanding. These connections were lifelines, offering empathy and strength when I needed it most.

Through these emotional landscapes, I discovered an inner strength I never knew I had. Motherhood, particularly for a preterm baby, was more than just a role; it was an all-encompassing experience that reshaped my very being. It taught me about the complexities of life, the power of love, and the importance of embracing every moment, no matter how challenging it might be.

The Body's Journey

Recovering physically and regaining health after the preterm birth of my baby was an intricate process. It extended beyond the usual post-delivery healing, involving unique challenges due to the early arrival. This section of my story discusses my physical recuperation, tackling postpartum symptoms, and tailored rehabilitation exercises.

It underscores the importance of good nutrition, ample rest, and regular medical consultations during my recovery. Here, I offer insights and advice from my experience to support and guide other mothers in enhancing their health and well-being in the post-preterm birth period.

Physical recovery after delivering my preterm baby was a path I walked with patience and care. Every part of my body seemed to have been transformed by the experience of early childbirth. The exhaustion was more than physical; it seeped into my bones, a constant reminder of the ordeal we had been through. Yet, each day brought a new awareness of my body's strength and resilience.

I learned to listen to my body, giving it the rest and nourishment it so desperately needed. Meals became more than just eating; they were moments of replenishing my strength and healing. The journey back to physical health was slow but steady, with exercises recommended explicitly for postpartum recovery. Each stretch and walk felt like a step toward reclaiming my physical self.

Regular medical check-ups were crucial. They monitored my healing and helped me understand the changes my body was undergoing. During these visits, I found reassurance in the knowledge and guidance of healthcare professionals.

But more than the physical recovery, the realization of my body's capability and resilience stood out. This physical healing process was also a journey of appreciation and respect for my body's incredible resilience, a testament to the strength inherent in motherhood.

Becoming Friends with Your Baby

Often, parents are so swamped and tired in the first few weeks that they forget to stop for a minute and absorb the fact that they have created a life. This is a beautiful occasion, and getting to know your baby's needs and likes is an incredible journey. We will discuss how to become friends with your baby for a better relationship for the whole family.

I vividly recount the early days of parenthood, which were filled with wonder, challenges, and an overwhelming sense of responsibility. I learned to understand and interpret my baby's unique cues and signals during this phase.

I discovered that every baby has a language, a unique way of communicating their needs and emotions. They often start with cries, which can vary in intensity and tone, each carrying a distinct message: hunger, discomfort, or simply the need for closeness. Through attentive observation and countless comforting moments, I began to decode these cries, responding with the appropriate care and attention.

But it wasn't just about the cries; my baby communicated through subtle gestures and expressions. From how his eyes followed me to the gentle grasp of his tiny fingers, I learned to recognize these nonverbal cues. Responding to these cues wasn't just about meeting his physical needs and building trust and understanding between us.

Feeding, bathing, and playtime were not just routine activities; they were the threads that weaved the fabric of our connection. I learned to sync with my baby's cues and needs through these everyday moments. Feeding became more than just nourishment; it transformed into a sacred time when our eyes met and our hearts connected. Bathing became a joyful ritual filled with giggles and splashes, strengthening our bond with each splash and laugh. Playtime was more than just fun; it was a window into my baby's world, filled with wonder and curiosity.

Fostering a serene and affectionate atmosphere for my baby went beyond the physical space; it was about enveloping my baby in emotional warmth and a profound sense of security. I discovered that the ambiance I created was just as important as the care I provided. The softness in my voice, the gentle touch of my hand, and the peacefulness in our surroundings all contributed to an environment where my baby felt safe and cherished.

This emotional cocoon was essential for his development and our deepening bond. It became a sanctuary of love where we could nurture our relationship, one cuddle at a time. We prepared him a colorful baby cot with soothing music, which he often enjoyed, especially when satisfied.

I reflect on the invaluable significance of two crucial elements in my journey of connecting with my baby: patience and presence.

Patience became my constant companion as I embarked on this path of motherhood. It wasn't just about waiting for my baby to settle into a routine or those first smiles; it was about understanding that every step of our relationship was gradual. It required patience to decipher his needs, to soothe his cries, and to witness his growth. Patience wasn't just a virtue but the foundation upon which our bond was built.

Equally essential was presence, both physically and emotionally. Being there for my baby was more than just being in the same room; it was about fully engaging in every moment we shared. It meant setting aside distractions and savoring each interaction, from those late-night feedings to the quiet moments of cuddling. My presence was a reassuring constant in my baby's life, a source of security and comfort.

Together, patience and presence formed the cornerstone of our connection. They allowed me to be attuned to my baby's needs, to respond with love and care, and to create a profound understanding between us. In this section, I explore the profound impact of these qualities in nurturing a solid and lasting bond with my baby.

A happy and connected baby becomes a beacon of joy, radiating positivity and harmony throughout the home. Their laughter becomes the family's soundtrack, and all celebrate their milestones. This newfound happiness, born out of a deep parent-child bond, can uplift spirits and give the family a sense of completeness.

As parents, my spouse and I found that our strengthened bond with our baby enhanced our relationship. The shared moments of caring for and connecting with our child have brought us closer, reinforcing our relationship. We embarked on a journey together, sharing the joys and challenges and strengthening our connection as a couple.

Beyond the immediate family, the impact extended to grandparents, aunts, uncles, and close friends. Our baby's infectious happiness had a ripple effect, fostering a sense of unity and connection among extended family members. Everyone was eager to participate in this journey, contributing to the understanding of communal joy.

Keeping Your Head Above Water

It would not be a balanced look at being the parent if we did not speak about those times when you feel as if you are drowning and cannot cope. Those nights when you do not get any sleep because the baby is crying constantly and the long days that follow when the baby will not eat can be incredibly stressful for parents. We will look at practical ways to cope with situations arising from having a preterm baby.

I vividly recall those sleepless nights when my baby's cries seemed never-ending. The exhaustion was relentless and often felt like no relief in sight. These were the nights when doubts crept in, I questioned my ability to soothe my baby, and the weight of responsibility pressed heavily on my shoulders. During these moments, parents may find themselves navigating uncharted waters, feeling lost and overwhelmed.

The long days, followed by persistent feeding struggles, added to the stress. The worry and anxiety about whether my baby was getting enough nourishment were constant companions. The feeling of helplessness can be overwhelming, and during these times, it's easy to forget that asking for help is a sign of strength, not weakness.

I want to share the practical strategies that were my lifeline during these challenging moments. Seeking support, not only from my spouse but also from a network of friends and family, became essential. We leaned on each other for strength and shared the weight of the challenges, fully understanding that we were in this together. Additionally, I discovered that self-care wasn't just a luxury but a lifeline that allowed me to replenish my reserves to continue providing the best care for my baby.

Seeking Support

One of the first and most crucial steps I took was seeking support. Parenthood can be an overwhelming journey, especially with a preterm baby, and trying to navigate it alone can feel like an impossible task. I turned to my spouse and opened up about my feelings and struggles. We became a united front, supporting each other emotionally and sharing the responsibilities of caring for our baby.

Beyond our relationship, I contacted a network of friends and family. They became my pillars of strength, offering a listening ear, a helping hand, and a sense of community. I realized I didn't have to go through this journey alone; a support system was ready and willing to help.

Leaning on Each Other

Parenting is a team effort, and I learned that leaning on each other was vital for our family's well-being. My spouse and I divided tasks and responsibilities, recognizing that we both had unique strengths and abilities to contribute. We shared the load, from feeding and diaper changes to comforting our baby during those long, sleepless nights.

This division of labor lightened the individual burden and strengthened our bond as a couple and as first-time parents. It reminded us that we were in this together, facing the challenges as a united front.

Embracing Self-Care

Self-care emerged as a lifeline during this journey. I discovered that taking care of myself was not a selfish act but a necessary one. It allowed me to recharge physically and emotionally, which is essential for providing the best care for my baby.

My self-care routine included quiet reflection, mindfulness exercises, prayer, and short breaks where I could step away and recharge. It was a delicate balance between caring for my baby and preserving my well-being. Self-care became a way to replenish my reserves and continue caring for my baby with patience and love.

Building a Support Network

Beyond my immediate family, I also found strength in building a support network of other parents who had experienced similar challenges. Connecting with other parents of preterm babies provided an invaluable sense of camaraderie and understanding. We shared our stories, offered advice, and provided emotional support to one another. These connections fostered a sense of community and reminded me I was not alone on this journey.

Seeking Professional Help

In some instances, the challenges of parenthood, especially with a preterm baby, can become overwhelming. During these times, seeking professional help, such as counseling or therapy, can be crucial. I learned that there is no shame in seeking the guidance of a trained professional to navigate complex emotions and challenges. This decision ultimately helped me gain clarity, perspective, and coping strategies.

These practical steps were instrumental in helping me navigate the trying situations that often arise from having a preterm baby. They served as anchors, grounding me during the stormy moments of parenthood and reminding me that I had the strength and support to keep my head above water.

Conclusion

In the intricate tapestry of parenthood, Chapter 8 has been a journey through the uncharted territory of emotions, physical recovery, and the art of building a profound bond with a preterm baby. The chapter paints a complete picture, acknowledging this unique voyage's highs and lows, the triumphs and tribulations.

When a mother holds her preterm baby, an extraordinary transformation begins. The emotional adjustments are complex and filled with a symphony of joy, anxiety, love, and fear. This chapter has peeled back the layers of these emotions, validating the rollercoaster ride that new mothers embark on. It has illuminated the profound connections forged amidst the isolation, highlighting the incredible strength found in communities of mothers sharing similar experiences.

We've also journeyed through the physical aspects of recovery, understanding that the body's resilience is a testament to the wonders of nature. The chapter underscores the importance of self-care, rehabilitation, nutrition, and rest, which are the pillars of physical well-being that allow mothers to regain strength and health.

The heart of this chapter is the journey of becoming friends with your baby. We've explored the nuances of recognizing a baby's cues, establishing a communication rhythm, creating a nurturing environment, and understanding the roles of patience and presence. These elements are the building blocks of a deep, loving bond between parent and child.

As we conclude Chapter 8, we recognize that parenthood, especially with a preterm baby, is a profound and transformative experience. It's a journey filled with challenges and a trip where resilience and love shine brightly. Every tear, smile, sleepless night, and joyful moment contributes to the beautiful tapestry of family life.

CHAPTER 9

৩৩৩৩৩

PERSONAL SUPPORT SYSTEMS

One thing becomes abundantly clear in parenthood no parent is an island. Especially for mothers of preterm babies, the support system plays a pivotal role. The weight of nurturing, protecting, and caring for a preterm baby can be immense, and in this chapter, we delve into the significance of personal support systems. We understand that it's not only okay but essential to lean on others during this challenging journey. Let's explore the key aspects covered in this chapter, each contributing to the well-being of both parents and their precious preterm babies.

Letting Fathers be Hands-On

Mothers often feel it is their responsibility to be the sole provider for a baby. This is a lot of responsibility to take on their shoulders. They have carried and birthed the baby, and yes, it is lovely to be a mother, but mothers need to let fathers bond with the baby, too. We will discuss how allowing a father to be part of a newborn's aspects fosters a bond with the baby and gives the mother time to take a much-needed and deserved break.

Parenthood is a shared journey, and it's essential to recognize that both parents play a vital role in nurturing and raising their child, especially when the baby is preterm. While mothers have carried and given birth to the baby, fathers have a unique and equally important role in their child's life.

Allowing fathers to be hands-on caregivers fosters a solid and enduring bond between them and their babies. This bond is built through moments of feeding, diaper changing, soothing, and simply spending quality time together. It's a chance for fathers to connect with their children deeply and emotionally, creating a foundation of trust and love that will last a lifetime.

In our case, we were together in the theater during the caesarian delivery of our baby. He was there to receive the baby from the medical care team and dedicated him to God before handing the baby back to the medical care team. His presence in the theater was an assurance. After all, I wasn't alone in bringing the baby into the world. It gave me hope that we would jointly care for the baby.

While I was still in the ICU, he worked hard to pump the breastmilk from me and take it to the neonatal ICU for the baby to drink. He did this for the three days I was in the theater. He was not ashamed of moving around the theater with the breast pump and a cup to pick up the breast milk for our baby. Perhaps without his being there, our baby would have missed out on the colostrum, the richest first breastmilk needed to protect the baby against sickness.

Parenthood comes with many responsibilities, and sharing these responsibilities lightens the load for both parents. It's not about taking away tasks from mothers but rather about sharing the joys and challenges of caregiving. Fathers can actively ensure the baby's well-being, allowing mothers to take much-needed breaks for self-care and rest.

In the early days of my recovery from a C-section in the hospital, he continued to support me to sit and position the baby to effectively breastfeed without hurting my wound. Besides providing this breastfeeding support, he also carried and spoke to the baby as I rested in the hospital. This routine continued even after we left the hospital. I saw it as an opportunity to let the baby embrace his father as I rested.

Embracing an equal partnership in parenting sets a powerful example for the child. It conveys that both parents are equally capable and responsible for the child's care and upbringing. This partnership benefits the child and strengthens the relationship between the parents as they navigate the joys and challenges of parenthood together.

This was important in our case, especially during the times the baby was so irritable, for instance, when sick and having colic. We realized we had unique, effective ways of handling the baby during such difficult times. Therefore, being open to letting each parent play any role they are good at was an important lesson we learned, and it worked out well for us.

Involving fathers in caregiving strengthens the family unit. It promotes open communication, understanding, and teamwork within the family. When both parents actively participate in parenting, it creates a harmonious and supportive environment in which the child can thrive. There is no better time to start this than soon after the baby's birth. Fathers, for example, have deeper voices that are soothing and comforting to the baby. Thus, their active involvement in baby care is always crucial.

Some fathers might face cultural barriers to doing this, especially when it is unacceptable for husbands to carry out roles. My spouse did not have any such hindrances in our case, but I know some friends whose husbands cannot do that, especially in public. Thus, it is important to educate and positively influence fathers, boys, men, girls, women, and mothers to have fathers play essential roles in supporting their spouse's care for the babies beyond providing financial support.

Allowing fathers to be hands-on caregivers is not only beneficial for the child but also for the mother's well-being. It will enable mothers to take breaks, recharge, and prioritize self-care. Mothers can find comfort knowing they have a reliable spouse who can assist when needed.

Open and respectful communication between the mother and the father regarding the need for him to come in and support her is critical in making this a more pleasurable experience for the father. This helped us navigate our joint care for our preterm right from day one.

Letting fathers be actively involved in caregiving is a win-win for everyone involved. It nurtures a solid father-child bond, promotes shared responsibility, and strengthens the family unit. It's a testament to the idea that parenthood is a journey best undertaken together, with both parents playing essential and complementary roles in their child's upbringing.

There is no way I can forget how our baby got excited whenever we got to his court, with one holding each hand. I still have a video of him making beautiful giggles with the excitement of a baby who had an affirmation that both parents loved him equally and unconditionally.

When he learned to crawl, he often pulled us to his play area and demanded we sit together and play with the toys with him. This act was a powerful reminder that our child noticed and appreciated the firm foundation of joint parenting to him from babyhood. It reminds mothers and fathers that shared parenting should start as soon as the baby is conceived.

Allowing Family to Show Their Love

The arrival of a preterm baby can bring about a surge of work, stress, and sleepless nights that can be even more challenging than with a full-term baby. This section addresses the importance of including extended family, whether it's the baby's siblings or the parent's family, in the baby's life. By entrusting grandparents and other relatives with the care of the baby, parents can find moments to reconnect, rest, and regain their strength.

This section explores the emotional journey of letting go and allowing others to step in. We delve into the mental aspect of understanding that your baby will be fine without you constantly being there. We also touch on the challenges that may arise when family members add pressure instead of providing support.

In the whirlwind of parenthood, especially when caring for a preterm baby, having a circle of love and support is akin to having a safety net that gently cradles the family. It signifies the network of extended family members, including grandparents, aunts, uncles, siblings, and friends, who rally around the parents and the newborn. This circle of love and support is like a warm embrace that envelops the family during a time when every ounce of care and comfort matters.

It's a network of individuals who come together, not just out of duty but out of genuine affection and concern for the well-being of the baby and the parents.

It's a testament to the idea that parenthood is not a solitary journey but a shared experience within the larger family unit.

Within this circle, each member plays a unique role, contributing their love, care, and wisdom. Grandparents often bring the knowledge of experience and a deep well of affection, while aunts, uncles, and siblings provide additional layers of support and companionship. Together, they form a multifaceted support system that can help ease the burdens of parenthood.

Moreover, the circle of love and support is not just about providing practical assistance, such as helping with baby care or household chores. It's also about emotional support and creating an environment where parents feel understood, valued, and cherished. It's the reassurance that, even in the most challenging moments, there are loving arms to lean on and shoulders to cry on.

In the demanding and often overwhelming journey of parenthood, especially when caring for a preterm baby, finding moments for reconnection becomes not just a luxury but a necessity. This concept revolves around the idea that by entrusting the care of the baby to trusted grandparents and other relatives, parents can create invaluable opportunities for themselves.

These moments for reconnection are like oases in the desert of constant baby care. They offer parents a much-needed break from the round-the-clock demands of tending to their newborn. By allowing grandparents and other family members to take on caregiving responsibilities for a short time, parents can step away from their role as primary caregivers and focus on themselves as individuals and as a couple.

One of the significant aspects of these reconnection moments is the chance for parents to rediscover each other as a couple. Amid the sleepless nights, diaper changes, and feedings, it's easy for the relationship between spouses to take a backseat. These moments offer a pause, an opportunity for couples to reconnect emotionally, share their experiences, and enjoy each other's company.

It's a reminder of the bond that brought them together in the first place and a chance to nurture that connection. These moments provide a crucial opportunity for physical and emotional rejuvenation. Parenthood, especially in the early stages, can be physically exhausting. Finding time to rest, sleep, or self-care becomes essential for parents to regain their physical strength and emotional well-being. These breaks offer a chance to recharge, relax, and recover from the demands of caring for a preterm baby.

In the bigger picture, moments for reconnection are vital for maintaining a healthy and balanced family life. They contribute to the overall well-being of parents, enabling them to face the challenges of parenthood with renewed energy and resilience. Ultimately, these moments are a testament to the importance of self-care and the recognition that taking care of oneself is not selfish but a necessary part of being the best parents possible for their precious baby.

When caring for a preterm baby, finding moments for reconnection transcends being a mere luxury; it becomes an absolute necessity. This concept is anchored in the recognition that parents, who bear the immense responsibility of nurturing and caring for their newborn, need respite to recharge and rejuvenate.

These moments for reconnection serve as sanctuaries amid the relentless demands of baby care, offering parents a brief escape from the continuous cycle of caregiving. By entrusting the baby's care to trusted grandparents and relatives, parents temporarily relinquish their primary caregiver roles, allowing them to shift their focus back to themselves, both as individuals and as a couple.

One of the most profound aspects of these moments for reconnection lies in their capacity to rekindle the flame of love and relationship between parents. Amidst the unending series of sleepless nights, diaper changes, and feedings, the romantic relationship between couples can often become overshadowed. These interludes provide a well-deserved break, permitting couples to rediscover each other emotionally, share their experiences, and bask in each other's presence. These moments are a gentle reminder of the profound connection that initially brought them together, offering them the chance to nurture and strengthen this vital bond.

Furthermore, these respites offer a critical opportunity for physical and emotional revitalization. Early parenthood, particularly when caring for a preterm baby, can significantly toll a parent's physical well-being. Parents must replenish their physical stamina and emotional resilience when allocating rest, relaxation, and self-care time. These breaks serve as a platform for recharging, unwinding, and recovering from the strenuous demands of tending to a fragile, preterm baby.

In the grander scheme of things, moments for reconnection are indispensable for preserving a harmonious and healthy family life. They play a pivotal role in bolstering the overall welfare of parents, enabling them to confront the manifold challenges of parenthood with renewed vigor and unwavering resolve. Ultimately, these moments underscore the importance of self-care, emphasizing that taking care of oneself is not selfish but an indispensable component of being the best parents possible for their beloved baby.

Even with the best intentions, well-meaning relatives may inadvertently contribute additional pressure or offer unsolicited advice. Recognizing the importance of family involvement is vital, but it's equally crucial to acknowledge the potential complexities that can arise when various family members offer their input. It's a delicate dance of appreciating the support while gently asserting the boundaries necessary for the baby's and the parents' well-being. This was crucial in the early days when we were still in the hospital and upon taking our preterm home. We were under strict instructions by the medical care team to limit exposure of the baby to people until he was at least three months old.

This section guides parents, providing insights into effectively communicating their preferences and needs with extended family members. Ultimately, it underscores the value of fostering a collaborative and understanding family dynamic, where the collective goal remains the welfare and happiness of the baby and where each member plays a part in creating a nurturing environment for the entire family.

Friends for Life

Due to the social portrayal of how mothers are "meant to be," when we are not coping, we feel like we are failing a fundamental part of life. This is not so. Parenting a newborn is hard; parenting a preterm newborn can be exceedingly tricky. Having friends around whom you can speak honestly is especially important for a mother's well-being. We will look at loyal friends and how they can be a saving grace to the parent of a preterm baby.

In our society, there is often an idealized image of motherhood, one that portrays mothers as self-sufficient, nurturing, and always capable of handling any challenge that comes their way. This portrayal can create immense pressure on mothers to meet these unrealistic standards. As a result, many mothers feel compelled to present a facade of strength and competence, even when facing significant challenges.

The idea that seeking help or admitting struggles is a sign of failure stems from the misconception that a "good" mother should be able to manage everything on her own. There is a fear of judgment or criticism from others if a mother expresses vulnerability or seeks assistance. This fear can be paralyzing, preventing mothers from reaching out for the support they need.

Furthermore, societal expectations often downplay the difficulties of parenthood, especially when it involves caring for a preterm baby. It's common for mothers to internalize the belief that they should be able to handle everything without complaint. This can lead to isolation and guilt when encountering challenges beyond their control.

Parenting is a complex and multifaceted journey, and facing difficulties and needing help along the way is perfectly normal. Acknowledging our struggles and seeking support is a sign of strength, resilience, and a commitment to the well-being of our children. In this section, we aim to challenge and break free from these societal expectations, recognizing that true friends provide a safe space to be honest about our experiences without fear of judgment.

Indeed, true friendships can serve as a lifeline for parents of preterm babies, offering invaluable support and companionship throughout the journey of parenthood. These genuine connections provide a sense of solace, reminding us that we are not alone in our experiences. I remember my spouse sharing with his supervisor at work, who also happens to be a friend, about our preterm baby.

Having gone through a unique, challenging experience with her twins, she quickly activated her network and found us an excellent Neonatologist. This Neonatologist was swift in getting us the much-needed support from the early days while in hospital when we almost did not know what to do. Not only did she go on to become our friend, but she expanded our network of medical care team, who in turn have become our life-long friends. This is exemplified by Dr. Denis Muyaka, a pediatrician, and Dr. Victoria Nakibuuka, a consultant Neonatologist, who were there every step of our journey and have become our child's inspiration. Our child wants to become a medical doctor like them to help other parents and children.

One of the unique aspects of true friends is their ability to understand and empathize with the challenges we face. Annet, among my many friends, stood out during the early stage of my parenting journey. She left her comfortable home with her two equally young sons to care for me at my home. My nurse constantly massaged me, helped with stomach exercises, and shared her parenting stories. All these were important in getting me on my own feet.

True friends like Annet acknowledge that parenting, especially with a preterm baby, is a rollercoaster of emotions, and they are there to ride it alongside us. They offer a listening ear without judgment, allowing us to express our fears, anxieties, and uncertainties openly. Despite the difficult recovery I went through, Annet did not at any time complain or try to judge me.

She understood how difficult it was to have a caesarian section and a preterm and low birth weight baby at the same time. I recall the times she treated me like one of her children, enticing me to eat the not-so-favorable foods, including bitter tomatoes and spider plant 'cleome' vegetables. These are known to increase breast milk production.

Moreover, these friendships go beyond mere words; they are filled with actions that speak volumes. True friends extend a helping hand when needed most, whether babysitting for a few hours to provide a much-needed break or simply being present in times of crisis. Their support is unwavering, and their presence is a source of strength.

I cannot thank my friends, whether those I grew up with from my villages who have become sisters or those I met along the way in school or places of work who were there with me and my family every step of this journey of parenting a preterm baby.

Amid societal expectations and pressures, let us remember that true friends are the pillars of understanding and compassion. They remind us that seeking help, sharing our struggles, and admitting our vulnerabilities are not signs of weakness but courageous steps toward growth and resilience. As we delve into the significance of these friendships, let's embrace the comfort and reassurance they bring to our lives as parents of preterm babies.

The Significance of Authentic Friends

Authentic friendships during the challenging journey of parenting a preterm baby hold immeasurable significance. These genuine connections become a lifeline, providing emotional sustenance and a sense of belonging that can be transformative.

First and foremost, authentic friendships offer a safe and non-judgmental space for parents to express their feelings and share their experiences openly. When facing the complexities and uncertainties of caring for a preterm baby, the ability to confide in a friend who understands and empathizes can be profoundly comforting. It creates a sense of validation, assuring parents that their struggles are heard and their emotions are valid.

Moreover, these friendships serve as a vital source of emotional support. True friends provide a compassionate presence during the darkest hours, offering a shoulder to lean on when the weight of responsibility feels overwhelming. Their unwavering support reminds parents that they are not alone in their journey and that they can provide immense solace.

Authentic friendships also promote resilience and mental well-being. They offer a reprieve from the constant demands of parenthood, allowing parents to step away from their roles and be themselves temporarily. These moments of respite are essential for maintaining emotional balance and preventing burnout.

In summary, authentic friendships are significant because they can provide understanding, empathy, and unwavering support during the challenging times of parenting a preterm baby. These connections remind us that vulnerability is not a weakness but a testament to our humanity, and they empower us to navigate the journey of parenthood with greater strength and resilience.

Conclusion

We began by acknowledging the significance of fathers being hands-on parents, challenging traditional roles, and fostering a deep bond between fathers and their newborns. We explored the value of extended family involvement, understanding that caring for a preterm baby can be taxing, and allowing loved ones to provide support is a vital form of self-care.

We examined the invaluable role of friends who become faithful companions during the struggle, offering solace and understanding when societal expectations threaten to silence our voices. These friendships remind us that seeking help and admitting our challenges is not a sign of failure but courage.

In every facet of personal support, we found a common thread, a circle of love and support that envelops us in times of need. It's a reminder that parenthood is not a solitary journey but a collective endeavor, and by opening our hearts to the love and care of those around us, we can navigate even the most challenging circumstances.

As we conclude this chapter, let us carry forward the understanding that seeking help, accepting support, and embracing authentic friendships are not signs of weakness but demonstrations of our resilience and love for our preterm babies. These bonds and connections are the threads that weave the fabric of a strong and nurturing family, and they are the most authentic treasures on this remarkable journey of parenthood.

PART THREE

❧❧❧❧❧

SUPPORT SYSTEMS FOR MOTHERS OF PRETERM BABIES

CHAPTER 10

✤✤✤✤✤

CHANGES NEEDED IN OUTER SUPPORT SYSTEMS FOR MOTHERS

Preterm birth, a journey that commences earlier than anticipated, can be a profound and often unexpected turn in the odyssey of parenthood. In this focal chapter, we explore the critical role that external support systems play in shaping the experience of mothers who face the challenges of preterm birth.

We begin by understanding the role of healthcare professionals, who are often the first line of support. Their empathy, knowledge, and approach can significantly influence a mother's emotional and physical well-being. Here, we discuss the importance of being a supportive healthcare professional regarding medical expertise and emotional, psychological, and spiritual comfort.

The chapter then shifts the focus to the broader responsibilities of healthcare institutions. These organizations are more than just places for medical treatment; they are sanctuaries of hope and healing. We delve into how these institutions can adapt and evolve to meet the unique needs of mothers experiencing preterm births, including specialized care units, family-friendly policies, and comprehensive postnatal support.

A pivotal aspect of this discussion is the role of governments and other external organizations. Their policies, funding, and support programs are crucial in shaping the landscape of natal care. This section examines how these entities can create a more supportive environment for preterm births through funding research, developing supportive policies, and ensuring accessible healthcare.

Lastly, we address a frequently overlooked yet vital aspect: Men's roles in pregnancy, birth, and parenting in the context of preterm births. This section highlights the importance of inclusive support, recognizing fathers' emotional and practical involvement, and how they can be better integrated into the journey of preterm parenting.

In this chapter, we aim to weave a comprehensive picture of the societal, institutional, and personal changes needed to better support mothers during one of the most challenging yet transformative experiences of their lives. Our exploration is not just a call for awareness but a blueprint for action, urging all layers of the support system to adapt, empathize, and embrace their roles in this vital journey.

Being a Supportive Health Care Professional

Being a part of a woman's journey through pregnancy and birth is not just another aspect of medical work; it's a profound privilege. As healthcare professionals in Africa, where resources can be scarce and challenges manifold, this privilege carries an even more profound significance. We are not merely caretakers of health; we become integral parts of one of the most pivotal experiences in a woman's life. Especially when it comes to preterm births, the emotional landscape of this journey becomes even more complex and profound. It's even more critical for first-time mothers who end up with preterm births.

In our everyday practice, it's crucial to remind ourselves that pregnancy and birth, particularly a preterm one, are intensely emotional periods for parents and especially for mothers. In the African context, where cultural diversity and various beliefs about childbirth abound, our role transcends the mere provision of medical care. We become confidants, counselors, and sometimes the sole source of comfort for these mothers. We must navigate the physical health challenges and emotional and psychological terrain that these women traverse.

As we engage with expecting mothers, we must remember that each woman's story is unique. The journey is marked by its joys, fears, and expectations. For a mother facing the prospect of a preterm birth, the emotional load is heavy. Fear of the unknown, concerns about her baby's health, and the physical demands of a preterm birth are overwhelming realities. Therefore, our approach must be empathetic, patient, and understanding.

Communication is vital in this journey. It's not just about medical facts; it's about listening to her concerns, fears, and hopes. It's about reassuring her that she is not alone on this journey. We are there, not just as healthcare professionals but as pillars of support, guiding her through each step, explaining processes, and demystifying the complexities of preterm birth. I recall the fright in my wife's face at being told we were to have preterm delivery because of pre-eclampsia. I had a lot of anxiety with over a thousand questions to ask regarding the situation. Yet, I don't recall any doctor or other healthcare providers coming out to comfort and counsel us regarding what lay ahead.

In my experiences across different regions in Africa, I've witnessed the resilience and strength of women facing the challenges of preterm birth. Their strength often draws from the support we provide. Whether in a well-equipped hospital in a major city or a small clinic in a remote village, the essence of our support remains the same: to be present, empathetic, and a source of strength.

My commitment as a nutritionist and father to a preterm is not only to the physical well-being of mothers and their preterm babies but also to their emotional, psychological, and spiritual health. This commitment is a testament to the privilege of being part of such a significant phase in a mother's life. My role as a healthcare professional transcends professional duty; it is a profoundly personal and emotional journey intimately intertwined with the lives of the mothers I serve.

The Onus on Healthcare Institutes

The role of healthcare institutes in shaping the future of maternal and neonatal care cannot be overstated. There's a crucial need for a paradigm shift in the training provided in colleges, universities, and medical institutions, particularly in pregnancy, childbirth, and postnatal care. This shift must go beyond the traditional focus on the medical aspects of birth, extending to a holistic view that encompasses both mother and baby's emotional, psychological, and social well-being.

Healthcare education often leans heavily toward the technical and clinical aspects of care. While this is undeniably important, it is equally essential to integrate training that emphasizes empathy, emotional support, and understanding of childbirth's societal and cultural dimensions. The journey of pregnancy and childbirth, especially in cases of preterm birth, is laden with emotional complexities. Healthcare professionals must have medical knowledge and skills to navigate these emotional landscapes.

Moreover, a more robust curriculum that addresses the specific challenges and needs associated with preterm births is needed. This includes understanding the unique medical needs of preterm infants, the emotional and psychological support required by mothers, and the best practices for postnatal care. Training should also focus on interdisciplinary collaboration, ensuring that healthcare professionals can work effectively within a more extensive support network that includes neonatologists, psychologists, nutritionists, dieticians, social workers, and other specialists.

Another critical area for improvement is the accessibility and inclusivity of healthcare education. In many regions, especially in underserved areas, there is a shortage of trained healthcare professionals specializing in maternal and neonatal care. Addressing this gap requires increasing the number of training programs and making them more accessible to a broader range of students. This could involve offering scholarships, remote learning options, and outreach programs to attract and train individuals from diverse backgrounds.

Healthcare institutes also bear the responsibility of continuous professional development. Professionals must stay updated with the latest research, techniques, and best practices in the fast-evolving maternal and neonatal health field. This can be achieved through regular workshops, seminars, and refresher courses.

Healthcare institutes have a significant role to play in shaping a more supportive system for managing pregnancy and childbirth, particularly preterm births. By adopting a more holistic approach to education and training, fostering continuous learning, and increasing accessibility, these institutions can profoundly impact the quality of care provided to mothers and their babies. This shift benefits the immediate healthcare outcomes and has a lasting impact on society's overall health and well-being.

The institutes can collaborate better with training colleges, Universities, and medical schools to find ways to have evidence-informed updates on the latest innovations in maternal and childbirth, especially preterm birth. This will help keep all the relevant health workers informed of the developments and pass on the information to the mothers and caregivers with preterm births. Perhaps partnerships with social work and community psychology institutions could also add value, especially for the counseling and support of groups of individuals with preterm births, including women groups.

Governments and Outer Organizations' Role in Natal Support

In my experience working within the African healthcare system, I've seen firsthand how the involvement of governments and external organizations is crucial in shaping natal support. Government funding and policies, especially for public hospitals and clinics, are pivotal in determining the quality of prenatal and postnatal care available to mothers.

As a healthcare professional, I've observed that with more funding, significant improvements can be made in training staff on the ground, particularly in managing pregnancies and ensuring the health of mothers and babies. This is where the role of the Ministry of Health in various African countries becomes critical. These ministries allocate resources and set policies directly affecting maternal and neonatal health. Through my interactions with different health systems, it's clear that there is a need for these ministries to prioritize and promote better healthcare for expectant mothers, as well as enhance post-natal care facilities and programs.

However, support for natal care in Africa isn't limited to government efforts. Non-governmental organizations (NGOs) and international bodies like the United Nations supplement the government's efforts. In many regions I've worked in, these organizations have been essential in filling gaps in healthcare services. They provide resources, expertise, and global perspectives to address complex health issues. Their work in raising awareness, advocating for policy changes, and providing direct assistance to mothers and infants has been invaluable.

One critical aspect I've noticed is the importance of collaboration between government bodies and external organizations. When governments partner with NGOs and international agencies, the impact on maternal and neonatal health can be profound. Such partnerships can lead to better training programs for healthcare workers, more comprehensive maternal health campaigns, and improved care for mothers and their babies.

In my career, I have witnessed the successes and challenges of these collaborative efforts. Successful models often involve clear communication, shared goals, and a deep understanding of the local context. However, there are areas where improvement is needed, particularly in ensuring that these collaborations are effectively managed and adequately funded to meet the specific needs of each region.

Reflecting on my experiences in the African healthcare sector, I can see that the combined efforts of governments, NGOs, and international organizations are essential for providing comprehensive natal support. Through these collaborative efforts, we hope to see significant advancements in the care and support provided to expectant mothers and their infants across the continent.

Establishing and expanding functional NICUs across countries would support healthcare systems at all levels, including primary healthcare (PHC) facilities, and offer timely and quality care for mothers with preterm births. I have seen in Uganda, where there are functional, appropriately trained, and equipped health workers, there are many unnecessary deaths of preterm infants averted. The Ministry of

Health, on its own, cannot achieve this due to its budgetary constraints. So, partnerships with development partners, NGOs, and the private sector would be necessary.

Breast milk banks support preterm pregnancies, providing vulnerable infants with crucial nutrition and immunological protection. However, in most African countries, these facilities are non-existent, and there are no policy regulations or standards to support their establishment and operation. This lack of infrastructure and regulatory framework leaves many preterm infants without access to the life-saving benefits of donor breast milk. Governments must develop and implement policies that facilitate creating and regulating breast milk banks.

Development partners and the private sector must collaborate to fund and establish these facilities, ensuring they are accessible and meet international health standards. Additionally, raising public awareness about the importance of breast milk banks can garner community support and participation. Healthcare training institutes and regulatory bodies should also support providing specialty training in holistic care.

We also call on mothers to donate safe breast milk to support this critical cause. In Uganda, for instance, St Francis Hospital Nsambya, Nakasero Hospital, and Mbale Regional Referral Hospital have established breast milk banks. By contributing to these banks, mothers can help ensure that every preterm infant has the best possible start in life, significantly improving their chances of survival and long-term health. Through collective action and support, we can build a stronger, healthier future for all our children.

In developing countries, particularly in Sub-Saharan Africa, the role of registered nutritionists and dietitians in maternal and newborn care is not adequately recognized, especially within the private sector, where most preterm deliveries occur. Despite their critical importance, specialized training in lactation counseling and support for Neonatal Intensive Care Units (NICUs) and post-discharge care is almost non-existent.

Both government and private healthcare sectors must incorporate registered nutritionists and dietitians as integral members of the core care team. This inclusion would ensure comprehensive nutritional support for mothers and their preterm infants, improving health outcomes and reducing neonatal mortality rates.

Furthermore, healthcare training institutes play a crucial role in building the competencies of nutritionists and dietitians. These institutions should develop and implement specialized curricula focused on the nutritional needs of preterm infants and lactation support. By equipping nutrition professionals with the necessary skills and knowledge, healthcare training institutes can enhance the quality of care provided to preterm infants and their mothers, ultimately contributing to better health outcomes and reducing the burden of preterm births in the region.

Advocating for improved labor laws to provide more paid leave for parents in cases of preterm pregnancy is crucial. Preterm births demand extended medical attention and emotional support, necessitating extra time for parents to care for their newborns and manage the associated stress. Enhanced paid leave would allow parents to focus on their family's health and well-being without the added burden of financial strain, promoting better outcomes for both the child and the parents.

In addition to extended paid leave, it's essential to provide breastfeeding facilities at work. These facilities would enable mothers of preterm infants to continue adequately caring for their babies even after returning to work. Access to dedicated breastfeeding spaces ensures that mothers can maintain their milk supply and support their preterm babies' nutritional needs, fostering better health outcomes and reducing the risk of complications.

By incorporating both extended paid leave and workplace breastfeeding facilities, we can create a supportive environment that prioritizes the health and well-being of families dealing with preterm births.

Men's Roles in Pregnancy, Birth, and Parenting

Drawing from my personal experiences as a father to a preterm baby and as a man deeply involved in the journey of pregnancy, birth, and parenting, I can attest to the complex role men often find themselves in during this crucial phase of life. Our instinct as men, being doers, sometimes puts us in a position where, despite our best intentions, we may end up adding stress to pregnant women and new mothers.

To be candid, men cannot fully comprehend what a woman undergoes during pregnancy and childbirth. This gap in understanding often leads to a lack of empathy or appropriate care. This could have ramifications on the mother, the baby, and the father altogether. The consequences could get extreme depending on the strength of the relationship.

The truth is that our actions or inactions can exert considerable pressure on the women in our lives. When we fail to understand the emotional, physical, and psychological toll of pregnancy and childbirth, especially a preterm birth, we unintentionally contribute to their burden or worsen it altogether. This lack of understanding often stems from a societal structure where men are not typically encouraged or expected to engage deeply with the nuances of pregnancy, childbirth, and childcare.

For those who go through pre-marital counseling, some little bits and pieces are shared during pregnancy and birth. Even this little often vanishes without follow-up during pregnancy preparation, during pregnancy, and after maternity. This is especially true for first-time fathers and, more so, for the working class, who shoulder the burden of caring for their wives and babies.

As a Christian believer, I wedded in the first Pentecostal Church in Uganda, Makerere Full Gospel Church, where we received three months of premarital counseling by one of the senior pastors. Besides this counseling, we also attended church events for the married.

These conferences encouraged couples to find the best way to make their marriages work based on spiritual foundations and testimonies of couples who have made it through their marriages. However, there wasn't a single conference or counseling session for couples expecting their first baby or those with preterm babies.

It is good to note that there are men's and women's groups in our church whose motives are geared towards grooming complete men and women spiritually, physically, and emotionally. Based on this and other intricacies of pregnancy and childbirth, many men feel sidelined during this process, unsure of how to contribute meaningfully.

However, this narrative needs to change. We, as men, need to step up and become more involved, understanding, and supportive spouses. The first step in this journey is education and empathy. We must understand what pregnancy, childbirth, and childcare entail, not just superficially but sincerely, and appreciate our spouse's physical and emotional changes and challenges.

This can be achieved through attending premarital counseling, prenatal classes, the Marrieds'

Conferences, engaging in open conversations with our spouses, and seeking advice and insights from other experienced fathers and mothers. These opportunities are widespread, but we sometimes pass them on the pretext of being too occupied with other, more important undertakings.

We can't possibly have much more important undertakings than being present and connected to your dear spouse during pregnancy and childbirth. From a medical perspective, these are very risky stages of life that require delicate support. Failure to do so often comes with dire consequences, including the possibility of losing the lives of the mother and the child, a preventable experience no man would long to go through.

Moreover, being a supportive spouse extends beyond the pregnancy period. It involves active participation in parenting, sharing responsibilities, and providing emotional and physical support to the mother and the child. It's about being physically and emotionally present and connected and acknowledging that our role as fathers is as crucial as that of mothers. This includes understanding the needs of a preterm baby, which can be significantly different, more demanding, and more complex than those of a full-term baby.

For instance, the financial demands for preterm babies are much higher than for full-term babies. It's therefore necessary to have an appropriate financial plan for preterm birth to avoid additional emotional drain on the mother. If one is lucky enough to know the possibility of preterm birth, they would be better equipped. The cost of incubation in NICU and HDU, along with the daily necessities such as supplements, frequent hospital visits, and corrective surgeries, is unbearable for unprepared fathers. Those without medical insurance bear even the most tremendous burden in footing the hospital bills. This could destabilize and/or break up the couple's relationship if not well managed.

In my journey, I've learned that support comes in many forms. Sometimes, it's about doing the household chores to give my spouse some rest. Other times, it's about listening and providing emotional, physical, and spiritual support. Simple acts like providing her with the food she craves and regularly taking her out for fresh air, eating out, or simply walking together.

The truth is that pregnant women can have severe hormonal imbalances that affect their eating preferences or ability to freely interact with you and other people that they were once close to. It can quickly come out as offensive to you as a spouse, but we must understand that it's not her desire but the physiological changes contributing to this new experience. It's also about making informed decisions regarding the health and well-being of our children and their mothers.

Beyond pregnancy care, there's that critical care we need to provide during and after delivery. The simple act of escorting her to the delivery room for expected delivery or to the theatre for a C-section, as was our case, makes such a big difference in their lives and the childbirth outcomes and care. I demanded our medical team allow me to go to the theatre with her, and they graciously let me.

Besides the spiritual intercessions for successful surgery and birth outcomes, I was delighted to receive our preterm baby and to dedicate him to God immediately after he came out of the womb. Seeing the smile on the face of my spouse at the cry of our baby gave me joy and was an unforgettable moment. This is an experience I would wish for every man to have at all costs.

I also remember how much I stood in the gap, trekking between the ICU, where my spouse was admitted after the C-section, and the NICU, where our son was admitted to get his breastmilk. Whereas it looked strange in the eyes of many medical care teams and the rest of the patients, who were primarily women, I did it passionately, knowing it was a life-saving investment. Others may think this was out of no choice because we didn't have other immediate support. However, as a man, it was my responsibility to take charge and do the best for my spouse and child at the time; they needed me the most.

Perhaps the 'strangest' action I did, at least in the eyes of the conservative African men, was to nurse my spouse in the ward once she was discharged from the ICU. Not only did I feed her, but I bathed her and played a role often done by our mothers-in-law and aunties. I had all the possible excuses to give so that someone else could step in and play this role, but I couldn't, for it was the moment I reminded her we were in the situation and found ourselves together.

My support extended beyond the hospital to our home, where I continued with my full parental and spousal role. From the married perspective, I had to realize my spouse wasn't the same person she used to be during the preconception and childbirth period. She was bruised and had emotional and physical scars, which I had to appreciate and come to terms with.

For instance, she had a permanent C-section scar across her abdomen, which potentially could change how I saw her as that beautiful girl. It could have affected our romantic life mainly because I always wished she would deliver normally and avoid the C-section scar.

I remember she also got her hand deeply cut while caring for Jair. I had to understand she was healing from the birth exhaustion and injuries that required time, yet I didn't go out of my way to seek an outside relationship for marital satisfaction. As an African man who has worked in different parts of the continent, it's not uncommon to hear of how men desert their spouses after childbirth in pursuit of other women who can give them all-around company.

As men, we have a crucial role in pregnancy, birth, and parenting. Our involvement should be active, empathetic, and informed. By stepping into this role wholeheartedly, we can alleviate some women's pressures and become the supportive spouses and fathers we aspire to be. This journey is not just about being a 'doer'; it's about being a loving and caring spouse, a confidant, and a co-navigator in the beautiful yet challenging journey of bringing a new life into the world.

We shouldn't be the reason for our spouses ending up with preterm but rather that reliable support system that ensures they enjoy pregnancy, childbirth, and parenting as we bring up the best children to bring joy into our lives. If we err in our pre-and antenatal care leading to preterm birth, we shouldn't worsen the situation by abandoning the mother and the preterm baby altogether.

African Maternal Support: Evaluating Pre-Birth and Post-Birth Care

In my professional journey through various healthcare settings across Africa, I've witnessed the spectrum of pre-birth and post-birth support available to mothers. This experience has given me a clear understanding of what is available and, more importantly, what is lacking or not readily accessible in Africa.

Pre-Birth Support

Regarding pre-birth support, many urban areas in Africa have relatively good access to prenatal care. This includes regular check-ups, ultrasound scans, and access to some level of maternity education. However, the scenario is starkly different in more rural or underdeveloped areas. Women often lack access to primary prenatal care, which is crucial for monitoring the health of both the mother and the unborn child. Health education, which is vital in preparing expectant mothers, is also limited.

While undergoing pre-service training at the university, I remember we learned the need for at least six months of preparation for pregnancy. The reality is different in practice. Women and men do not have the slightest knowledge of the need to adequately prepare for pregnancy, including ensuring adequate weight gain, treatment of any underlying sicknesses, and other predicaments. This exposes the mothers to a high risk of pregnancy and birth complications, including preterm birth.

Another significant gap in pre-birth support is the lack of psychological counseling and emotional support for expectant mothers. Pregnancy, mainly when it involves complications like the risk of preterm birth, can be a stressful experience. Yet, the focus in many African healthcare settings remains predominantly on physical health, with mental well-being often overlooked.

From experience, it's common for pregnant women, even to the last stage of pregnancy, to indulge in a heavy workload. Pregnancy takes a toll on the woman, and the increased workload worsens the situation. With this fact, little support is indeed extended to such pregnant women to reduce their engagement in laborious work. I know of some mothers who unfortunately lost their lives and those of their babies due to heavy workloads.

Similarly, in my line of work, I have seen lots of preterm and low birth weight births attributed to heavy workloads. This is primarily true in rural areas. It's also happening in urban areas among the working-class pregnant women involved in demanding work schedules in organizations with poor human resource policies, which grant them adequate time to rest and take care of their pregnancies.

Post-Birth Support

Post-birth support, especially for mothers of preterm infants, is even more critical. While some specialized facilities in bigger towns and cities offer neonatal intensive care units equipped to handle preterm births, such facilities are scarce, often overwhelmed, and financially out of reach for ordinary parents.

Even within urban areas, medical insurance, which is usually the primary source of funding for the services, limits the amount of money spent on NICU. In rural areas, the situation is more challenging, with a severe lack of neonatal care facilities, postnatal care for mothers, and follow-up services to monitor the development of preterm infants.

Breastfeeding support and nutrition counseling, crucial for the health of both the mother and the baby, are also areas where support is limited or non-existent in many parts of Africa. Hadn't been a professional nutritionist, we would've fallen victim to the wrong breastfeeding advice and guidance from the nurses supporting us with our preterm birth. These nurses, although good-intentioned to save the life of our preterm, were advising me to initiate the baby on infant formula immediately after birth. The mother, having delivered the baby by C-section and having been admitted to the ICU, created in them the conviction we couldn't get breastmilk for the baby.

I kindly turned down their advice and went ahead to express the breastmilk from the mother of our preterm. This left me wondering how many of the hundreds of deliveries in this prestigious hospital and many more others out there are denied an excellent start to life through breastfeeding due to misinformation from health workers!

Additionally, postpartum psychological support is rarely available despite the high emotional toll that childbirth, particularly a preterm or complicated birth, can have on a mother. The little support provided to postpartum mothers and fathers is often purely medical. It is geared towards ensuring the mother completes the immunization and other mandatory services as prescribed by the Ministry of Health.

Although mental health and psychosocial support are critical to the success of caring for preterm babies, these have not received the relevant attention they deserve in Africa. This is unfortunate given the magnitude of mental health issues that come along with preterm birth, not just to the mother but to the father alike.

The Role of Community and Traditional Practices

In many African communities, traditional practices and community support play a significant role in pre-birth and post-birth care. While some of these practices are beneficial, others may lack the backing of scientific healthcare and can sometimes be detrimental to the health of the mother and baby.

For instance, it's common in Buganda, Uganda, to give babies *ekyogero*, an herb composed of clay and other ingredients, to treat colic, among other claims. This has no scientific backing and instead exposes babies, especially preterm ones, to sickness. Integrating beneficial traditional practices with modern healthcare and ensuring safe and effective maternal care is a complex challenge that remains to be adequately addressed.

While there are pockets of excellence in maternal care in Africa, a significant disparity exists between urban and rural areas. The lack of comprehensive pre-birth and post-birth support, especially in remote regions, highlights a critical need for enhanced healthcare infrastructure, better training for healthcare providers, and a more holistic approach to maternal care that includes both physical and mental health and psychosocial support.

Conclusion

As we draw Chapter 10 to a close, reflecting on maternal care in Africa, I am struck by the profound responsibilities and opportunities that lie before us. This journey through the various facets of support systems, from healthcare professionals to governmental and organizational roles and the crucial involvement of men in pregnancy and parenting, has been enlightening and humbling.

We have traversed the landscape of maternal support in Africa, uncovering its strengths and shortcomings. We've seen the critical need for more holistic, empathetic approaches in medical training and practice and the imperative for healthcare institutions to broaden their scope of care beyond the clinical to the emotional and psychological needs of mothers.

The role of governments and external organizations has also been brought to the fore, highlighting the importance of policy, funding, and collaborative efforts in shaping an environment conducive to the health and well-being of mothers and their babies. It has become clear that concerted, well-coordinated efforts are essential to bridge the gaps in maternal and neonatal care, especially in the face of preterm births.

Perhaps most revealing has been the discussion around the role of men in this journey. It reminds us that the narrative of pregnancy and childbirth is not solitary; it's a shared journey where the understanding, empathy, and active involvement of men can significantly alleviate the challenges faced by women.

In my personal experience, the resilience and strength of African mothers, the dedication of healthcare workers, and the potential of impactful policies and community support are the cornerstones upon which better maternal and neonatal care must be built.

This chapter is not just a reflection on maternal and neonatal support in Africa; it's a clarion call for action. It urges every maternal and neonatal health stakeholder healthcare provider, policymaker, development partner, community leader, or family member to play their part in weaving a stronger, more supportive net for the mothers and children of this vibrant continent.

As we conclude this chapter, let us carry forward the lessons learned and the insights gained. Let us commit to continuous learning, empathy, and action for the health and well-being of mothers and their children, which is the foundation upon which the future of our communities and our continent rests.

CHAPTER 11

ᚖᚖᚖᚖᚖ

CHANGING MINDSETS

O ur understanding of medicine, technology, and science has advanced tremendously in this modern era. Yet, when it comes to perceptions about pregnancy, birth, and particularly preterm babies, many outdated mindsets persist. Chapter 11 plunges into the heart of these lingering beliefs and attitudes, aiming to challenge and change them.

We live in a world where scientific breakthroughs and societal progress have revolutionized many aspects of our lives. However, certain deep-rooted beliefs about pregnancy and childbirth remain unaltered and continue to influence how we perceive and handle these life events, often to the detriment of those directly involved.

This chapter will address and critically analyze these mindsets, focusing on three key areas that are pivotal in shaping our understanding and approach to childbirth, especially in the context of preterm births.

Babies Are Women's Work: This section will tackle the long-standing belief that the care and responsibility of babies fall solely on women. It will explore how this notion not only undermines the role of men in parenting but also adds an unnecessary burden on women, particularly in the case of preterm babies who require specialized care.

There Is Something Wrong with Me and My Preterm Baby: The second aspect we will examine stems from the stigmatization and guilt often associated with preterm birth. Many mothers grapple with feelings of inadequacy and blame fueled by misconceptions about preterm births. We will dissect these feelings and the societal attitudes that contribute to them, offering a more compassionate and informed perspective.

Having a Baby is Natural; What's All the Fuss About Having a Preterm Baby?

The final part of this chapter will address the belittlement of the challenges associated with preterm births. It aims to enlighten and educate about the complexities and nuances of preterm births, contrasting them with full-term pregnancies to highlight why special attention and care are crucial.

Through this chapter, we aim not just to inform but to transform how societies, families, and individuals perceive and approach the journey of pregnancy and childbirth, particularly emphasizing the unique challenges of preterm births. It's a call to shed the old layers of misunderstanding and embrace a more inclusive, empathetic, and supportive mindset.

Babies Are Women's Work

In the first significant aspect of Chapter 11, "Babies Are Women's Work," I reflect on the deep-rooted mindset that has long influenced the roles of men and women in child-rearing, especially in the context of rural Africa. This belief, entrenched in tradition and cultural norms, suggests that the care and nurturing of children is predominantly if not exclusively, a woman's responsibility.

In many families, women are the primary providers of food and care, and this responsibility often extends unquestionably to the upbringing of children. However, this perspective overlooks the crucial role fathers and other male figures can and should play in their children's lives.

The notion that babies are solely a woman's domain stems partly from biological realities; after all, it is women who carry the baby and are typically the primary source of nutrition through breastfeeding. Yet, this biological aspect has been extrapolated to a broader social expectation that all aspects of childcare fall within the woman's purview. This mindset not only places an unfair burden on women but also deprives children of the rich, diverse nurturing that the involvement of both parents can offer.

The implications are significant in rural African settings, where this belief is often more pronounced. Women, already managing the demanding tasks of providing for the family, are left to navigate child-rearing complexities single-handedly. The challenge becomes even more daunting in the case of preterm babies, who may require additional care and attention. The absence of paternal support in such scenarios is not just an added strain on the mother but can also impact the well-being and development of the child. This could come as a direct impact of maternal mental health sickness.

These practices and attitudes also vary from community to community across African countries. The social norms entrenched in different cultures can't be underestimated. I remember way back in 2008, while working in a rural community in the Acholi region in northern Uganda, men wouldn't indulge in anything to do with direct care and support for pregnant and breastfeeding women. Upon doing my investigation, I learned that Acholi culture forbids men from getting too deep into maternal issues, including escorting their spouses to the hospital. This is worse in Karamoja, northeastern Uganda, where the man's role is strictly towards conception.

Once the woman has conceived, the man in the original traditional setting would desert her for the next wife, who is neither pregnant nor breasting. He would only return once the baby is about two years old, and the cycle gets repeated. Mind you, the

Karamoja sub-region in Uganda has the highest level of low-birth-weight babies, which is closely related to maternal pregnancy complications, including inadequate care. This is true in other parts of Africa where maternal care is insufficient for various reasons, including detrimental social norms.

Therefore, it's imperative to challenge and change this old mindset. Men need to be encouraged and supported to take an active role in their children's lives from the earliest stages. This involvement goes beyond financial support; it's about being present, engaged, and emotionally connected. The role of a father or a male caregiver in a child's life is invaluable; their engagement can have lasting positive effects on the child's emotional, social, and cognitive development.

Changing this mindset requires a collective effort. It involves educating communities, redefining cultural norms, and providing platforms where men can learn about and embrace their roles in childcare. It's about showing that caring for a child is not just 'women's work' but a shared responsibility that enriches the family.

As a father, I've experienced the profound bond that forms when a man actively participates in his child's life. This connection transcends traditional roles and contributes to a more balanced, nurturing, and supportive family environment. This change is beneficial for the child and the mother and transformative for the father.

Therefore, the belief that 'babies are women's work' is a mindset that needs to be reevaluated and reshaped. It's time to embrace a more inclusive understanding of parenting, where both parents share and celebrate the responsibilities and joys of raising a child.

This shift is essential for the immediate family and the broader societal fabric, as it paves the way for more empathetic, engaged, and balanced future generations. It's a foundation for building stronger and morally grounded nations globally. It's achievable if everyone gets involved, including spiritual, cultural, and other leaders all over the continent.

It isn't impossible to achieve it through an authoritarian and prescriptive approach to male engagement, as has been the case with the Ministries of Health and some civil society organizations. Evidence-based consultative approaches that see men and fathers as allies and not simply spectators in finding solutions would be needed.

This would also require programs targeting women to intentionally engage men. This will require multiyear, multisector, and actor engagement, including possible campaigns using men as champions of change and advocacy in maternal and childcare.

Is there Something Wrong with Me and My Preterm Baby?

Understanding the profoundly personal nature of this section, inspired by my own family's journey with our preterm child, I approach the topic of "Is there Something Wrong with Me and My Preterm Baby?" with both professional insight and personal empathy. The birth of our preterm baby was a pivotal moment, not just in our lives as first-time parents but also in shaping my understanding of the emotional challenges faced by families in similar situations.

The misconception that a preterm birth indicates a failure in the mother or an inherent problem in the baby is a distressing and sadly common belief. This mindset can cast a long shadow over what should be a time of bonding and love, replacing joy with unwarranted guilt and anxiety. As a father and healthcare professional, I've seen how this belief can unnecessarily exacerbate the emotional turmoil of an already challenging situation.

Preterm birth is more common than many realize, and it's important to emphasize that it is often a result of complex, multifactorial issues, most of which are beyond anyone's control. It's not a reflection of a mother's worth or capability, nor does it imply any inferiority in the baby. For instance, preterm birth could result from acute infection of the mother, pre-eclampsia, and depression, which, although preventable and manageable, could be beyond one's control. Thus, it's unfair to criticize them for the intended outcome of preterm birth, especially if you don't have the entire history.

Most preterm babies grow into strong, healthy children, defying the initial hurdles they face. We saw how, with appropriate care, including feeding, play, stimulation, and routine medical checks, our baby gained weight and grew into a very handsome and active baby. When anyone sees him today, they would have no idea he was a preterm birth unless they knew the history beforehand.

In our journey, my wife and I grappled with these feelings of self-doubt and concern for our preterm baby. The fact that none of us comes from a family with any history of preterm birth was even more disturbing and almost caused us to believe the sentiments that those around us had concerning our baby. To stay sane, we engaged in a process to shift our mindset, to understand that this was not a reflection of failure but rather a different beginning to our child's life story. This change in perspective was crucial in how we approached our roles as parents and supported our children's growth and development.

For instance, I used my professional expertise to ensure we had the right food supplements and provided diverse and nutrient-rich foods to him throughout his early childhood, which lasted from six months. This was critical in helping him gain the necessary weight and achieve the specific growth and development milestones despite his preterm delivery with low birth weight. While the mother concentrated on being the best mother she could be in terms of breastfeeding and taking care of him, I supported her with chores and other relevant tasks to reduce her workload.

A robust support system needs to be in place to help mothers change their thinking about themselves and their preterm babies. This includes medical care but also mental and psychological support and education. Mothers need reassurance and affirmation that their experience, while unique, is not an anomaly and certainly not a fault. Support groups, counseling, and access to accurate information about preterm birth can play a significant role in transforming these negative perceptions.

Furthermore, it's vital to celebrate the milestones and strengths of preterm babies, acknowledging their resilience and the remarkable growth journey they embark on. We made it a point to consistently measure and review our son's weight and other developmental milestones monthly. Any gain in grams, increase in length, or positive change in the growth and development milestone, such as crawling, made a huge difference in our lives.

We celebrated each milestone, for it reminded us that we had done our very best to support our preterm son in growing into a physically stronger and exceptional gift to us and the world. Unlike many parents who keep their children's growth and development milestones in the child health cards after every monthly visit to healthcare providers, we took ours too seriously by celebrating all the positive gains.

As parents, we found strength in the support of our medical team, our family, friends, and our community, which helped us see beyond the initial fears and uncertainties. Our medical team, including the Pediatricians and nurses, provided us with medical care and solid psychosocial and mental health support throughout our journey. We never felt judged by any of them at any time, but rather, they motivated us by acknowledging the progress we made with our son.

They were only a phone call or a physical visit away in case we needed to get any support with our baby. Of course, the physical visit to the hospital was draining, given the long distance and the heavy traffic jam we had to navigate not less than six times a month. At times, we wished those medical teams worked in the closest hospital to save us the long distance and exhaustion that came with the physical visitations.

Our family members, including the elderly female housekeeper, supported our journey. Whether massaging my wife's stomach or her swollen feet, they were always there and understood our predicament. Susan, our house helper, and elderly mother understood that my wife was a young first-time mother who needed support. She treated her like her own daughter.

"Buy me mango seedlings, and I will plant trees for the baby in the womb to enjoy when he is born," Susan requested me. Today, that mango tree, which we call Jair's Mango, stands tall in our compound as a reminder of Susan's selflessness in caring for us and our baby.

Aunt Beatrice, sister Annet, and many other family friends became our daily source of motivation in parenting our preterm baby. We also relied on our parents and relatives to provide the necessary support. This journey wouldn't have been easy with them.

The journey of parenting a preterm baby is filled with unique challenges and emotions. As we explore this mindset in the chapter, shifting the narrative from blame and deficiency to understanding, support, preparedness, and resilience is essential. Our experience as parents of a preterm baby has taught us the importance of compassion and education in overcoming these misconceptions, paving the way for a healthier, more positive approach to this unique journey.

For parents who are spiritual like us, we often relied on prayers to gain supernatural wisdom, healing, and direction when caring for our preterm became difficult to comprehend humanly. We frequently had prayer sessions for ourselves and our preterm baby in our house. This helped us to stay connected to God and gave us the confidence that our son would be all right, irrespective of the preterm birth.

Having a Baby is Natural, What's All the Fuss About Having a Preterm Baby?

In addressing the third aspect of Chapter 11, "Having a Baby is Natural: What's All the Fuss About Having a Preterm Baby?", I draw from my experience as a parent of a preterm baby and my professional background. This perspective has given me a deeper understanding of the unique challenges that parents of preterm babies face, challenges often not fully comprehended by those who haven't lived through them.

There's a common belief that having a baby is a natural process that parents instinctively know how to navigate. While there's some truth to this regarding the natural bonding and caregiving instincts that kick in, the reality of caring for a preterm baby is vastly different and more complex than that of a full-term baby. The needs of preterm infants are often more critical and demanding, and the journey for parents is laden with unique challenges and pressures.

From the intense environment of the neonatal intensive care unit (NICU) to the round-the-clock care required at home, the journey with a preterm baby is challenging to prepare for fully. As new parents to a preterm baby, my wife and I quickly realized that the traditional expectations and norms associated with newborn care did not apply to our situation. Our baby's early arrival meant facing a host of medical, growth, and developmental challenges that were both daunting and emotionally taxing.

Educating those around us about the realities of having a preterm baby became an essential part of our journey. It's crucial to create awareness and understanding of what it means to have a preterm baby, not to elicit sympathy but to foster empathy and support. Sharing our experiences, the challenges we faced, and the specialized care our baby required helped our friends, family, and the community understand why this journey was different and needed different support and sensitivity.

Furthermore, this education is not just for the immediate social circle of parents with preterm babies. It extends to the broader community, healthcare professionals, development partners, the private sector, researchers, program managers, and even policymakers. By raising awareness, we can advocate for better resources and support systems for parents of preterm babies. This includes access to specialized healthcare, mental health, and psychological support for the parents and creating a supportive community network.

This discussion aims to bridge the gap in understanding and create a supportive environment for parents embarking on this journey. It's about acknowledging that while having a baby is a natural process, traveling with a preterm baby has its complications, complexities, and demands. By sharing our stories and educating those around us, we can contribute to a more informed, empathetic, and supportive society for parents of preterm infants.

I have learned that many of these people are out there who urgently need accurate and reliable information that can work in their situation and context. In today's fast-moving internet world, there are all kinds of misinformation that can be detrimental to preterm babies. Therefore, experiences from parents like ourselves become valuable and more practical for parents of preterm babies to adapt to their context.

As we complete, we aim to highlight the unique experiences of parents with preterm babies. It's a call to shift perceptions, expand our understanding, and build a supportive network that recognizes and addresses the unique needs of these families. Our journey with our preterm baby has taught us the immense value of awareness, empathy, and community support, and it's these values that we hope to propagate through this discussion.

Conclusion

Reshaping our perceptions around pregnancy, birth, and particularly the experience of having a preterm baby is both necessary and great. This chapter has investigated the practical aspects of these experiences and an introspective journey into the societal and personal beliefs that shape our responses to them.

The discussions on the outdated notion that 'Babies Are Women's Work,' the misplaced feelings of guilt in 'There Is Something Wrong with My Preterm Baby and Me,' and the misunderstanding in 'Having a Baby is Natural; What's All the Fuss About Having a Preterm Baby?' have all pointed to a common need for deeper awareness and empathy. As a father of a preterm baby and a witness to the journey my wife and I undertook, I have seen firsthand the impacts of these mindsets and the importance of challenging them.

The path to changing these mindsets is not straightforward. It requires continuous effort, open dialogue, and a willingness to confront and unlearn deep-seated beliefs. It involves educating parents, families, healthcare providers, and the broader community. Through this education and awareness, we can build a more supportive environment for all parents, especially those facing the unique challenges of preterm birth.

Moreover, this chapter has highlighted the importance of inclusivity in parenting roles, the need for destigmatizing preterm birth, and the critical understanding of the specialized care required for preterm babies. These insights are not just theoretical; they are lived experiences that demand our attention and action.

In conclusion, "Changing Mindsets" is more than a chapter in this book; it reflects a movement towards a more understanding and supportive society. As we close this chapter, let us carry forward the lessons learned, the empathy gained, and the commitment to support and celebrate every journey of parenthood, no matter how unique it may be. Our experience, particularly in the African context, underscores the urgency and necessity of this shift in perspective. It is a shift that can transform experiences, improve outcomes, and enrich the lives of parents and children alike.

CHAPTER 12

ᕦᕦᕦᕦᕦ

LOOKING AHEAD

In "Looking Ahead," the concluding chapter of our exploration, we delve into three pivotal subsections that encapsulate the essence of our journey with a preterm baby. "This Too Will Pass" serves as a poignant reminder of the transient nature of life's challenges, offering hope and perspective to those amid their parenting journeys.

"It Takes a Village to Raise a Child" revisits the timeless wisdom of communal support, highlighting the invaluable role of the community in nurturing and supporting both the child and the parents. Finally, "Social Responsibility to Share Your Experiences" emphasizes the profound impact of sharing personal stories, encouraging parents to contribute their unique voices to a collective narrative of strength, empathy, and support.

This Too Will Pass

"This Too Will Pass." These simple words contain profound truth, especially when viewed through the lens of parenting a preterm baby.

My journey as a parent of a preterm child has been a testament to this reality. The countless sleepless nights, constant worry, and relentless care cycle often felt endless, as if they had become permanent fixtures of my life. Yet, as I reflect, I realize the impermanence of those intense early days and the importance of mental resilience and support.

I would be a liar to say we didn't have those moments where we would break down upon seeing how tiny and vulnerable our son was then. Not forgetting how much additional pain he was in when confronted with bloating or when he fell sick and the nurses couldn't locate his blood vessels for injections. Seeing an already vulnerable child in pain in the backdrop of already injured mental health creates more challenges than solutions in the journey of caring for preterm babies.

When you're facing yet another sleepless night like we did, it's easy to fall into the trap of believing this is your new normal. The world shrinks to the confines of your baby's needs, and time seems to both stand still and rush by in a blur of feeding, comforting, and monitoring. In these moments, the mental toll can be as challenging as the physical demands. It's a period marked by a rollercoaster of emotions, from profound love and protective instincts to overwhelming exhaustion and anxiety.

However, it is crucial during these times to hold onto the understanding that this phase, like all others, will pass. This understanding doesn't negate the moment's difficulty but offers a beacon of hope, a reminder that change is inherent to life. Keeping a mental balance is key. It involves acknowledging your feelings, allowing yourself to experience a range of emotions without judgment, and reminding yourself that these challenges are not permanent.

We reached a point where it seemed normal and okay for us to acknowledge the difficulty in managing a preterm baby. It was more complex in the earlier days when we had just returned from the hospital, as we had not yet come to terms with the reality of having a preterm baby. There were moments when we didn't know what to do and instead traded blame for the situation. The sooner we realized we needed to accept the situation and acknowledged that it was temporary, our journey of parenting our preterm baby became joyous.

Having the proper support is also vital in navigating this journey. Support can come in various forms from a spouse, family, friends, healthcare professionals, community members, or parent support groups. These networks provide practical assistance, emotional support, understanding, and, sometimes, a much-needed respite. Sharing experiences with others who have been through similar situations can also be incredibly comforting. Knowing that others have walked this path and emerged from it can be a powerful source of strength and hope.

Most importantly, it's about constantly reminding yourself that these early, demanding days are not forever. There will come a time when sleepless nights give way to restful ones when the constant worry eases into a more manageable rhythm of life. As parents, we gradually find our footing, learn to adapt, and develop resilience we never knew we had.

In retrospect, as tricky as those early months were, they were also filled with moments of indescribable joy and love. The first smile, the first time they grip your finger, each little milestone becomes a celebration, a testament to both the baby's strength and your own. I can never forget the first giggles our son made a few months after we brought him home. It was comforting and a powerful reminder that we had overcome the most critical stage in the growth and development of our preterm baby.

"This Too Will Pass" is a mantra and a reality. It's a reminder to hold on, seek support, and trust in your resilience and that of your baby. The journey of parenting a preterm baby is undoubtedly challenging, but it is also replete with moments of profound growth and unexpected joy.

This subchapter guides navigating through the toughest times with the knowledge that these challenges are obstacles and footholds to a future filled with unique rewards and a special kind of love.

It Takes a Village to Raise a Child

Historically, in many African cultures, a child's upbringing has been a communal effort, with the responsibility shared among extended family members, neighbors, and the wider community. This collective approach has provided a robust support system for parents and a rich, diverse environment for children to grow up in. However, in modern times, both in Africa and globally, our lifestyles have become more individualistic, often leading to isolation in parenting experiences.

Despite these changes, communal support in child-rearing remains crucial. African communities still have a strong sense of collective responsibility towards children's welfare. Neighbors and extended family members often step in to provide care, advice, and support, reflecting a deeply rooted belief in the communal role of child-rearing.

This support is particularly vital for parents of preterm babies, who may face additional challenges that require not just emotional but also practical support. I can't recall how many visitors we received at home to check on the little one and comfort us upon delivering preterm. Often, such visitors don't visit without any gift for the child or the mother; seeing and taking nothing is against African values. During such visits, we received enormous support, including education and counseling on dealing with preterm birth.

In contrast, in many parts of the world outside Africa, especially in Western societies, the concept of communal child-rearing has diminished significantly. Nuclear families often live far from extended relatives, and neighbors may not share the same close-knit relationships seen in traditional African communities. This shift has led to a greater need for structured support systems for new parents, including those with preterm babies. It calls for reimagining community support in a modern context, where formal support groups, parent networks, and community-based initiatives become essential to fill the gap left by the erosion of traditional communal structures.

Recognizing the social and moral responsibility to support parents and mothers in need is critical in African and international contexts. African communities must preserve and strengthen the existing communal support structures, ensuring they adapt to the changing times while retaining their core values. Internationally, the focus may be more on building these support systems and fostering community through shared experiences and mutual aid.

This involves not just the participation of individuals but also the involvement and engagement of community leaders, healthcare providers, and policymakers. Creating awareness about the unique needs of preterm babies, providing platforms for sharing experiences and knowledge, and advocating for policies that support family welfare are all part of building a supportive community.

Moreover, in African and international contexts, technology and social media can play a pivotal role in bridging the gap created by physical distances. Online support groups, virtual consultations with healthcare professionals, and digital platforms for sharing experiences can offer new ways to connect and support each other.

Health facilities and healthcare providers, alongside information management experts, have a central role in documenting and connecting the parents of preterm babies to existing networks of support groups within their localities. Every day, there are new preterm babies born in different cities across the continent whose parents struggle with coping with such births. Imagine the health facilities developed a database of preterm births with their location and contact details. It would become more accessible for healthcare providers and other mental health and psychosocial support experts to follow up and care for them through groups and networks. Borrowing from the concept of community prayer cells as used in churches could be a good starting point.

In conclusion, "It Takes a Village to Raise a Child" reminds us of our collective responsibility toward society's youngest and most vulnerable members. Whether in the close-knit communities of Africa or the more dispersed familial structures elsewhere, the need for a supportive community in raising children, especially those born preterm, is universal.

By embracing this communal spirit and adapting it to fit our modern lifestyles, we can ensure that all children receive the love, care, and support they need to thrive regardless of where they are born.

Social Responsibility to Share Your Experiences

Sharing personal journeys, particularly those involving the challenges and triumphs of parenting a preterm baby, has an insightful impact. My experience has taught me the immense value of shared stories, not just in healing and processing our own experiences but also in providing guidance, comfort, and hope to others.

Having another parent who has walked the same path as yourself by your side is such a powerful reminder that, after all, you are not the first or the last to go through the challenges that come with preterm birth. It encourages us to pick up the broken pieces and do our very best to care for our preterm babies with love while enjoying the gift of parenting.

The journey of parenting, especially under circumstances as delicate as preterm birth, is often riddled with uncertainties, challenges, and a profound sense of isolation. The thought frequently crosses our minds during these times: "I wish someone had told me about this!" This sentiment underscores the importance of sharing our experiences.

As parents who have navigated the complex path of raising a preterm baby, sharing our story becomes not just a personal act of reflection but a social responsibility, a gift of immense value we can offer to others in similar situations. This worked very well in helping improve the positive living with HIV and AIDS, where the infected persons openly came out and spoke about their condition. It also helped reduce the stigma against people living with HIV and AIDS in Africa and elsewhere.

Knowing the high level of stigma that exists against parents of preterm babies and the children themselves, we can adopt the same approach and provide safe spaces for willing parents to come out and share their experiences freely. It will create champions of change for preterm births and strengthen the support for their parents, hence enhancing the growth and development of their children.

Sharing experiences goes beyond merely recounting events; it's about imparting the lessons learned, the emotional challenges faced, and the strategies that helped us cope. It's about offering a glimpse into the reality of the situation, including the fears, the joys, the setbacks, and the triumphs. This sharing can be incredibly powerful, especially for new parents of preterm babies who feel overwhelmed and underprepared for the journey ahead.

By sharing our stories, we can provide a sense of solidarity and understanding that is often missing in generic advice or medical explanations. Personal narratives bring a human touch to neonatal care's usually clinical and daunting world. They offer real-life insights that can help others in the same predicaments set realistic expectations, prepare for potential challenges, and feel less alone in their experiences.

Whereas there are expert clinicians who offer excellent medical support, many of them haven't gone through the realities of preterm births. From our journey of preterm birth, we can confidently say having real-life experience sharing with parents who have walked the same journey becomes more valuable in filling the gap that medical advice can't.

Additionally, sharing our experiences can be a form of outreach to those who may not have received the support they needed during their journey. It's an opportunity to offer what we might have received in terms of support or to give what we desperately needed but did not have. We help build a community of empathy, support, and collective wisdom.

It's also important to recognize that sharing experiences isn't just beneficial for those receiving the information; it can also be a cathartic and healing process for the sharer. It allows for a processing and understanding of one's journey, a way to find meaning in the challenges faced, and a pathway to healing and growth. This is exactly what we went through, and nowadays, we are always eager to share our stories with new parents of preterm babies.

In our increasingly connected world, there are numerous platforms through which we can share our stories. The avenues are diverse, from support groups and online forums to blogs and social media. Each narrative shared becomes a thread in a larger tapestry of collective experience, contributing to a more informed, empathetic, and supportive community.

This is a call to all parents, especially those with the unique experience of raising a preterm baby, to share their stories. It's an invitation to contribute to a more significant dialogue, to help demystify the journey for others, and to create a more supportive environment for future parents.

In sharing our experiences, we help others and contribute to our healing process. After all, we are only as significant as the amount of ourselves we give to others, the power of shared experiences, and the communal bond they foster in parenting.

To share this experience, an enabling environment from the government and support from healthcare institutions, development partners, civil society organizations, cultural institutions, and the private sector is necessary. Beyond equipping the healthcare facilities with the relevant equipment and human resources to provide specialized care for preterm babies and their parents, there is a need for financial and other technical support to enable the documentation and sharing of the experience widely with different audiences using several media platforms.

Conclusion

As we draw Chapter 12 to a close, let us reflect on the journey that has been traversed, not just in the pages of this book but in the lives of those who have walked the path of parenting a preterm baby. With its focus on the future, this chapter brings together key insights and lessons that transcend the immediate challenges of preterm birth, offering a broader perspective on the journey of parenthood and the role of the community in this journey.

In "This Too Will Pass," we explored the transient nature of the early, intense days of caring for a preterm baby. This section served as a reminder of the resilience inherent in parents and children, highlighting the importance of perseverance and hope. Though daunting now, the sleepless nights and relentless worries gradually give way to more stable, joy-filled times. It's a testament to the enduring strength of the human spirit and the incredible capacity for growth and adaptation in the face of adversity.

In "It Takes a Village to Raise a Child," we revisited the timeless wisdom of communal support in raising children. This subchapter underscored the importance of community involvement and engagement, particularly in modern times where traditional support structures may have weakened. Whether in the close-knit communities of Africa or the more dispersed social structures elsewhere, the need for a supportive network remains crucial. It's a call to action for society to rekindle the spirit of collective child-rearing, ensuring that every child, especially those born preterm, receives the care, love, and support they need to thrive.

Finally, "Social Responsibility to Share Your Experiences" highlighted the profound impact of sharing personal stories. This sharing is not just an act of generosity towards others but also a step towards healing and growth for oneself. By sharing our experiences, we contribute to a culture of empathy and understanding, providing guidance and support to those embarking on similar journeys.

"Looking Ahead" is not just a conclusion to this chapter but an ongoing narrative that continues beyond the confines of this book. It's a narrative of hope, resilience, and community we can shape and enrich as members of society, parents, and individuals.

Let us carry forward the lessons learned, the empathy gained, and the connections forged. Let us continue to support, share, and grow, not just for ourselves but for future generations. Parenting a preterm baby, with all its challenges and joys, is a profound reminder of our shared humanity and the incredible capacity for love and resilience within each of us.

CONCLUSION

As we conclude *Born Too Soon: A Guide to Coping with Preterm Birth*, we reflect on the key themes and messages that have resonated throughout the book. This journey, chronicled by Alex and Stella Mokori, has been an intimate exploration of the multifaceted experiences of having a preterm baby. From the initial shock and adjustment to the joy and growth that comes with it, each chapter has offered insights, guidance, and support.

The book began by sharing the authors' backgrounds, connecting with the readers, and setting a foundation for understanding their journey. We explored the importance of pregnancy preparation, the reality of not always reaching full term, and the myths versus facts of different birth methods. The birth of a preterm baby, the unique challenges it brings, and the journey of getting to know and care for this new life were discussed in depth.

The book's emphasis on personal and external support systems was central. We delved into the crucial roles of healthcare professionals, institutions, and communities in providing comprehensive care and support. The book also challenged traditional mindsets and highlighted the importance of shared responsibilities in parenting.

"Looking Ahead" was a powerful final chapter, reminding us of the impermanent nature of challenging times and the significance of communal support and sharing experiences. It reiterates that while having a preterm baby is difficult, it is also a journey filled with learning and unexpected rewards.

In closing, "Born Too Soon" leaves parents with a message of hope, resilience, and the importance of community and empathy. It's a tribute to the strength of parents and children alike and a reminder that you are never alone in the journey of preterm birth. It's also a reminder to everyone, whether in government, development agencies, the private sector, civil society organizations, research institutions, or others that we all have a critical role in making preterm birth acceptable and joyous for every parent. When added up with others, your small actions make a huge, lasting impact on the lives of parents, preterm babies, and the generations to come. There's no action too small; do it today.

ABOUT THE AUTHORS

⊷⊷⊷⊷⊷

Alex Mokori is a professional nutritionist with over fifteen years of progressive experience in public health and nutrition programming across various international non-governmental organizations (INGOs) and the United Nations Children's Fund (UNICEF) in Uganda and Africa. My journey in nutrition is deeply rooted in personal and professional experiences, shaping my unwavering dedication and passion for improving the lives of children and women through better nutrition.

I hold a Doctorate in Human Nutrition from the University of Pretoria, South Africa, a Master of Science in Applied Human Nutrition from Makerere

University in Kampala, Uganda, and a Bachelor of Science in Human Nutrition from Sokoine University of Agriculture in Morogoro, Tanzania. These academic achievements have equipped me with a robust foundation in the science of nutrition, enabling me to contribute effectively to various public health initiatives and research endeavors to combat malnutrition and enhance health outcomes for vulnerable populations.

Over the past decade and a half, I have been privileged to work with some leading public health and nutrition organizations. My roles have spanned from direct program implementation to strategic planning and policy development. I have been honored to contribute to numerous projects to address malnutrition, enhance food security, and promote sustainable agricultural practices. My work has taken me to diverse communities across Africa, where I have witnessed firsthand the challenges and triumphs in the fight against malnutrition.

My early life experiences profoundly influenced my journey into the field of nutrition. After losing my biological mother at a tender age, my paternal grandmother breastfed and nurtured me during my formative years. This experience instilled in me a deep appreciation for the critical role of nutrition in early childhood development and survival. Unsurprisingly, I found my calling in the nutrition sector, where I can channel my compassion and commitment into meaningful work supporting children and families.

I am passionate about empowering others to be the best they can be. This passion drives my work and interactions with colleagues, community members, and the individuals and families we serve. I believe in the transformative power of education and support, and I am dedicated to helping others realize their potential and achieve better health outcomes through improved nutrition.

As a proud father of a preterm son, I have a personal stake in the issues surrounding preterm care. This experience has heightened my awareness and advocacy for the needs of preterm infants and their families, reinforcing my commitment to ensuring that every child has the best possible start in life, regardless of the challenges they may face at birth.

This book is a culmination of my professional expertise and personal experiences. It aims to provide a comprehensive guide for parents, caregivers, and healthcare professionals navigating the complex world of preterm care. Through this book, I hope to share valuable insights, practical advice, and a message of hope and resilience. Together, we can significantly impact the lives of preterm infants and their families, ensuring a brighter and healthier future for all.

❧❧❧❧❧

Stella Mokori was born in 1988 in Nyakishonjwa, Kyeshero, Kayonza, Kanungu District. She was the second of three daughters in a family of eight and enjoyed a vibrant childhood. Raised by teachers, Stella was a spirited child with a strict Headmaster father who prioritized education above all else. From an early age, it was clear that she would be given every opportunity to excel academically.

Her educational journey began early, thanks to her parents' profession, and she had the privilege of attending good schools. Despite having multiple siblings in school simultaneously, Stella's determination remained unwavering despite the financial constraints. She completed her high school education and joined Makerere University, which was a significant 560 kilometers away from home. The distance underscored the importance of her mission: to complete her degree without delay, retakes, or distractions. She understood that there was neither time nor money for second chances.

Stella holds a Master of Business Administration from the Cyprus Institute of Marketing and a Bachelor of Commerce degree with a major in Accounting from Makerere University, Kampala. Over the past 11 years, she has gained progressive experience in finance, accounting, grants management, and operations within the private sector and international non-governmental organizations (INGOs).

Her passion extends beyond her professional life. Stella is deeply committed to childcare, striving to groom children into the perfect image of God. She believes in the transformative power of nurturing and educating young minds. Additionally, she has a profound appreciation for good food, which brings joy and balance to her life.

Stella's journey is a testament to resilience, hard work, and unwavering commitment to personal and professional growth. Her story is one of inspiration, dedication, and the relentless pursuit of excellence, making her an invaluable co-author and spouse in the creation of this book.

⤙⤙⤙⤙⤙

www.ingramcontent.com/pod-product-compliance
Lightning Source LLC
Chambersburg PA
CBHW032151080426
42735CB00008B/666